Echoes in the Stars

Gordon Frisbie

TFL Stories
https://tflstories.com

For Mom, Sara, and Yoshi

In memory of my father
and all the adopted souls
who wait inside my heart

Think of a mind as a sea. Its own inland sea. We can connect to
the enormity of others, the sea in them. We can connect to Dog.
Hound of the Ocean as the ancients once said.

Eileen Myles

He spoke with tears
Of fifteen years
How his dog and him
Traveled about

Jerry Jeff Walker

PREFACE—EXPLORING THE HEAVENS

A few years after stumbling into the new millennium, I was surfing the internet on my work computer and came upon a website that challenged me with its claim of superior deductive ability. It prompted visitors to think of an object— any object. The omniscient algorithm would then open a portal into their minds before probing their consciousness with twenty questions. Only two responses were required: yes or no. At the conclusion of this mind-meld, the clever cyber-sleuth would triumphantly identify the mysterious object.

While several technical reports had yet to be completed, I played the game anyway. I selected a common household item and tried to be honest with my replies. Near the end, the inquiry became personal.

"Do you put it in your mouth?"

Of course I did. The curious entity was showing a high degree of intelligence. I clicked the "Yes" button. There was a long pause. The virtual luminary was extrapolating my answer. Then it posted a final question: "What is it?" After submitting my response, I received a very dogmatic reply: "You don't put a dog toy in your mouth." Perhaps I should use my hands while playing tug-of-war with my pups, but my teeth provide a strong grip and a better chance at winning.

Although I'm more of a dog person than a people person, I usually don't read dog stories. My friends will recommend books about our four-legged soulmates, and I will politely thank them and file their suggestions under "maybe someday." Over the years, I have received many of these as presents or recommended reads and have yet to crease the spines on most of them. All the same, I have enjoyed a few classics like *White Fang, Call of the Wild, The Dog Who Wouldn't Be*, and maybe a couple more.

To be honest, dog stories can make me sad. While they might contain an entertaining wealth of companionship, excitement, mystery, terror, love, bravery, and humor, there's a good chance they'll conclude with loss and heartache. The satisfaction of reading a really good story can be doused by my sympathy for the hero.

Then Boo came into my life. And then she left me with too many memories. I didn't want these to fade, so I wrote them down. After several months, this adventure evolved into a manuscript. Despite my neurotic disposition toward this genre, it was the perfect vehicle for my stories.

Rather than a simple biography or memoir, I've quilted together snippets and sketches from our past to create a whimsical tapestry. She was the common thread that bound precious fragments of time within my thoughts.

Overall, I wanted to capture the inspiration she brought into my life. I hope these memories and ruminations will paint a vivid picture of Boo, her cohorts, and the world we all shared together.

I have tried to avoid a sad ending. That's the type of dog story I would enjoy. All dogs go to Heaven. They have no original sin to worry about. On the other hand, bunnies might go to Heaven as well. But when they get there, they must wonder what they did wrong.

The story about the first seasons of Boo's life may always be a mystery. It's likely she lived for more than sixteen years. We celebrated fifteen adoption days and the folks at Denver Dumb Friends League assumed she was one year old when I adopted her.

She was my first dog and only child. My life as an egocentric bachelor came to an end. It was an abrupt and unplanned transition. I suddenly emerged upon a strange planet filled with new priorities and responsibilities.

For example, I've never enjoyed walking alone at night. This is probably true for most folks. For Boo, though, nothing was more exciting than exploring the dark nighttime world. She quickly earned my trust and was allowed to run freely during our evening walks. Then a vibrant unknown world emerged from the shadows.

During the day, the sky was a mirage of blue and white. On clear nights, the mirage disappeared and was replaced by a boundless universe that exceeded my imagination. The infinite depth of a clear night sky was simultaneously humbling and magnificent.

Every evening, Boo and I wandered beneath the night sky. The solitude fused our souls. During the summer, it was more of a twilight sky until bats and nighthawks signaled the onset of dark nights.

And every morning, while it was still dark—with maybe a gunmetal fringe of daylight—we went outside so Boo could relieve herself. Above our heads, planets within our solar system glimmered like a line of incandescent pinholes. With stars and darkness slipping behind the veil of dawn, this was the best time to observe the sun reflecting off our celestial neighbors.

This was also the best time to collect a urine sample for our veterinarian. I would bring a kitchen ladle and shove it under Boo's butt as soon as she squatted. If the cold metal touched her nether parts, she would jump up and look at me like I was some kind of freak.

Without Boo, my nighttime walks are infrequent and brief. When I leave my home, I no longer have the confidence and excitement that once trotted by my side. My timid human psyche needs a brave companion when I venture into the dark.

At the same time, she's still with me every day and night. It's hard to put into words, but I've tried.

Thanks for listening.

RIDING HIGH

Six hundred feet below us, the deep-blue water and rocky shores of Cheesman Lake subdued the tumbling South Platte River before allowing it to continue down through canyons of ancient granite and gneiss.

It was an ideal late-summer day in the foothills of the Rockies. The graded dirt road on the north side of the lake split into two forks. I slowed down and parked my truck in the middle of the junction. As usual, Boo was the first one out of the truck as my door swung open.

Except for a black ear, black eye-patch, and black stub of a tail, she was a white Australian shepherd. Her coat was short, her waist was slim, and her legs were strong and fleet. With her head held high and droopy ears pointed forward, she relished the details of our surroundings.

Spastic hovering grasshoppers rattled the stillness with raspy chatter. I returned to the truck, drank from my water bottle, poured some into Boo's dish below her seat, and opened my map. The right fork looked more intriguing and this settled my decision about which road to follow. Boo remained at her post with rapt attention. She wasn't ready to hand the reins back to me. But there was more backcountry to explore farther up the road. I pointed to the open door and said, "C'mon. Let's go." She understood and jumped in. This would be a day of wonderful rewards.

Prior to this trip, agility trials in Colorado and Wyoming had consumed too many weekends. Everything had followed an elaborate plan. Competing was still in our blood and we would attend more events in the future, but now we had a chance to be dogs again.

When I turned the key, the engine sounded just like the grasshoppers: "Clickclick clickclick clickclick clickclick." Not good. I tried again. "Clickclick clickclick clickclick clickclick." My stubborn denial lasted for many iterations until our predicament became obvious.

Several hours later, I was heading east on Highway 285 as a passenger inside a tow truck. My only company in the cab was an extremely taciturn driver. The wind rushing past our open windows added a ruffling fury to the silence.

Boo was riding in the cab of my truck, which, in turn, was riding on the bed of the tow truck. Although she had a spectacular view, the vertical arrangement of the vehicles also created a high center of gravity. This should have been a concern for our driver, but it wasn't. He embraced the challenge of the downhill curves like a tipsy elephant on roller skates. My fingers dug into the edges of the vinyl seat while the tires chirped against our radial momentum.

As the mountains and foothills retreated behind us, I released my grip on the seat. The gentle contours of the western Great Plains concealed most of the metropolitan area. Distant clumps of tall buildings and skyscrapers affirmed our return to civilization.

We passed through new and old suburbs before being greeted, once again, by the South Platte River. After crossing the river, we ascended a gradual rolling slope into the cities of Englewood and Denver. Highway 285 became Hampden Boulevard and my spirit became remorseful. Fueling my melancholy, the driver maintained his silent demeanor while I stared at the familiar cityscape as it flowed by.

Even though my truck was securely chained to the bed of the tow truck, I often turned my head to reassure myself. Whenever her comical black-and-white face appeared above my dashboard, Boo seemed to be enjoying the ride. I could only hope this was true. Her steady focus created the illusion that she was piloting my crippled truck. This must have amused the other drivers on the road.

For all the miles, hours, and days Boo and I had shared on the road, complete sentences were infrequent and dialogue was inferred. This silence was never awkward. Our thoughts were never hidden. If she needed sympathy for her loyal endurance of boredom, she would lay one paw on my lap while her head and other paw rested on my knee. With the steering wheel rubbing the back of her neck and my hand scratching her shoulders, I would tell her we were almost there.

The tow truck climbed into the city and the horizon crept toward us. We were approaching the first small summit on the east side of the river. As we passed over I-25, a new vista arose. In the distance was a long green hillside where my townhome awaited us. Somehow this lifted my spirits. It had been a lousy trip for Boo and me. We were almost home.

The brooding driver dropped into Goldsmith Gulch while quietly pondering personal matters. An influx of vehicles from the highway and Monaco, combined with commercial zoning and punitive stoplights, hobbled our progress. A bumper sticker on an old GMC truck said, "Got My Chevy." Yeah, I thought, and I've got my dead Dodge.

Cycling through gears and silent observations, the driver crossed Goldsmith Creek and climbed to the top of another prominence. As we drove by a cemetery, our silence acquired a solemn aspect. Blocks of apartments and more commerce guided us into a wide and shallow valley. Cherry Creek Dam rose in the distance and disrupted the natural contours.

A wide curve, which swung away from the dam and onto

Havana Street, gave the driver one more opportunity to test the stability of his load. If he had ever shown any emotion, it was pure impatience.

Havana carried us over Cherry Creek and into Aurora. Following a brief discussion about local navigation, we turned onto Yale Avenue and began another eastward ascent along shady trees and covenant abiding communities.

Near the top of the grade, I interrupted the silence and said, "Turn left here." The driver obliged and we arrived home a few minutes later.

Boo remained confined inside my truck while the driver climbed onto the tow truck's bed, released the shackles, dropped back down to the ground, tilted the bed, reversed the winch, and rolled my truck into a vacant parking space. Before allowing him to conclude his business, I freed Boo and welcomed her shameless display of affection.

"Gotta keep moving. That'll be four hundred."

"Will you take a check?" I was still wiping my face.

"Sure."

NOTES ON COYOTES

A frequent character in my stories about Boo is the coyote. This critter is best described as a self-sufficient individual with antisocial tendencies. A pack of four coyotes would be a large gathering for these wild wallflowers. This personal observation, and several others, were verified using an accepted scientific method known as "walking the dog."

First, let's get the pronunciation right. Most folks say "ky-yo-tee." That's how I pronounced it until a group of professional wildlife scholars ridiculed my ignorance. In perfect unison, they chortled and shrewdly explained, "It's pronounced 'ky-yoat'." To prevent future embarrassment, I accepted their academic axiom. In fact, I like the efficiency of removing the third syllable. You will thank me if you ever run into a roaming pack of biologists.

Coyotes have burrowed deep into Denver and Aurora. With their gift of natural independence, they have adapted to surviving within the city limits while avoiding taxation. They go wherever they want, explore every unclaimed patch of real estate, and then move on. Far from being domesticated, they rely on wit and instinct to survive in a place where they find little sympathy.

When I moved to Aurora, I was familiar with the urban legends about the cunning and nefarious nature of coyotes. As will become evident where the coyote coyly sneaks into these stories, these myths are true. And over time, I would learn of their reluctant respect for the conviction and authority of a strong-willed dog.

In the early days of our evening excursions through nearby open spaces, Boo was allowed to travel no farther than the end of her leash. Occasionally I saw coyotes off in the distance and moving away from us. As Boo became more reliable, I allowed her to run free without a leash. Almost immediately, as an independent animal, she became a target for the coyotes. They had lost their fear of me as well and often passed by my knees as they approached my girl.

To ensure her safety while confirming my fashion awareness, I bought a spiked collar for Boo. It was pure Goth. She wore it during our nightly walks for several months until it was replaced with a sturdy leather collar that was more comfortable and durable. But my interference was mostly superfluous. Her fearlessness often discouraged any hostility.

One dark winter night, my attention was diverted elsewhere when I heard Boo's angry screams. She had been encircled by three coyotes. With threats on all sides, she constantly switched the angle of her defense. The coyotes were deliberate and persistent in keeping her surrounded. Like a bubble drifting with the wind, the assailants continued to push her away from me. I followed the edge of the circling pack with no concern for my own safety.

I attempted to assist Boo's reactions with obedience and agility commands, but the evolving tactics of the coyotes limited her responses. Even though the drama lasted no longer than this recollection, each second was distinct and dilated. With determined resistance, she finally held her ground. I ran to her side and secured her with a leash. Then the three hoodlums silently vanished into the night.

Coyotes look like dogs, but they are very different. Dogs have a more dependent nature because we've selectively bred individuals with this attribute. We depend on them, they depend on us, and the benefit is mutual. Some pups are less clingy than others, but there's a measurable amount of dependence in all dogs. The remaining portion of their spirit is an independent hunger that has never disappeared.

A wild coyote would be a terrible pet. They are beautiful creatures, especially in their winter coats, and have an admirable intelligence. But even if a coyote were groomed to eliminate unpleasant infestations and given a stupid name, its wild spirit may remain untarnished. And that's the way it should be.

Another difference between the two species can be seen in the tracks they leave in the snow. Coyotes will make clean "single-track" prints that often follow a straight path. Single-track walking conserves energy by using one paw print for each side of the body. As a result, the tracks look like those of a two-legged animal. And trotting in one direction with minimal deviations is the most efficient way to cover lots of territory.

Coyotes appear to travel with steady purpose. Their minds are focused upon a distant objective. Walking in a straight line across a field is not easy. Yes, I've personally investigated this matter. A fresh layer of snow is helpful for documenting the results. Initially, my tracks betrayed a confused agenda. Every slight turn of my head created similar detours in my path. I finally succeeded in mastering this folly by focusing on a single point in the distance. My ability to make perfect robotic trails still gives me great satisfaction.

When we stroll through open country, our dogs may single-track and move in a straight line to catch up with us. But it's more common for them to meander, follow their noses, and investigate hidden baubles.

Coyotes enjoy a more rounded diet than our kibble-fed friends. Although both species appreciate farmed or free-range meat products, coyotes will also feast on fruits like wild plums and chokecherries. In contrast, dogs rarely nibble on wild fruit, and when they do, only a few berries are harmed.

My knowledge of coyote food is based on frequent observations. They prefer to poop in the middle of the trail where I can examine it. This is not because they're lazy and rude—this is how they claim their territory. They take great pride in displaying their turds.

The indigestible portions of fruit, such as seeds and skins, are prevalent in late summer and fall. Rodent and bunny fur provide roughage for their winter diet.

Coyotes also have a slightly different posture than dogs. When at ease and standing, both have a similar profile, with a high head, a straight back, and, sometimes, proud ears and a bushy tail. But when we compare their ability to be slinky and sneaky, the coyote wins. Their slink is like that of a four-legged snake. Very few dogs can duplicate this stealthy posture.

And the coyote has no competition when it comes to looking like something from the gates of hell. My girl Boo had impressive hackles that ran the length of her back with a slight dip at her hips. A coyote's hackles, on the other hand, run from head to tail with no interruption. Then they will arch their backs to appear even more sinister. These wild dogs will also stretch their faces toward their necks until their heads resemble furry skulls. If a person were still inclined to keep one as a pet, this threatening apparition would give any salesman second thoughts.

My coyote neighbors are primarily nocturnal. This works to their advantage since they are nearly invisible at night (except when it snows). As evening falls into darkness, a joyful chorus of howls and yips can pierce the silence. Their day is just beginning and this is their wake-up call.

The rising sun will send them back to their dens or hideouts. Although we've seen many coyotes during the day, confrontations have been rare. They will often retreat into their shady homes as we draw near.

Social interactions among dogs and coyotes are limited by mutual snobbery. One species cannot understand how the other was included in God's plans. But, as with any perfect plan, there is an exception. These contradictions are known as "coydogs" and embody a strange bond of kinship between the two species. Like any classic romantic tale through the ages, coydogs symbolize the triumph of true love over tribal hostilities. In fact, over the years, Boo was courted by a few lover-boy coyotes. But she was not that kind of girl.

One morning Boo and I saw an animal that was one or two inches taller than a typical coyote and quite handsome. He embellished his coyote squeal with a throaty howl. That's what caught my attention. Until then, I had no belief in coydogs. Other folks have seen a similar creature in this same area. He has been described as quite shy and reclusive around dogs. It must be a strange existence for this wild mutt and he might suffer from bouts of instinctual confusion.

The coyotes I've seen in Denver and Aurora appear to be larger than those in more remote areas. This could be related to our abundance of rabbits and geese. Or maybe the local coyotes have a smidge of Fido inside them as well.

Regardless of their possible genetics, I've grown to have a fair amount of respect for my coyote neighbors. They have traveled, fought, hunted, and slinked to the top of the wild metropolitan food chain. In a strange way, I admire them and have moments of weakness when I ponder the possibility of a mangy *Born Free* experience.

PIEDMONT PRIMER

I grew up with dogs. Canine companionship goes back to my first memories. Despite this, I never owned a dog until I became a middle-aged human.

Before owning or being owned by a dog, I was drifting throughout the northwest and trying to earn a living with a college degree in wildlife and fisheries biology. Near the beginning of this odyssey, I was employed as a lab assistant at the Flathead Lake Biological Station in Montana. One of the resident graduate students, Burt, was averse to inactivity and always somewhere else. When he took a break from his exploits and joined us in the lab, we'd gather around and listen to his latest tale. Burt had a simple philosophy about life: live every day so you have a story to tell at the end of it.

Even though adventure is near the bottom of my daily priorities, there is wisdom and truth in these words, and I have applied them whenever possible.

Most of my expeditions have been within the forests and tundra of the Rocky Mountains. I've never lived in a state without mountains and alpine retreats are often within a reasonable distance. If my view doesn't include a soaring and jagged skyline, then there isn't a good reason to live there.

I was living in Aurora, Colorado when Boo came into my life. Initially I thought she would be the perfect companion for my trips into the hills. A slight adjustment was required for this fantasy. Boo's pink skin on her nose and around one of her eyes lacked protective pigmentation. Exposure to intense sunlight at high elevations severely irritated her eyelids. And even with daily applications of sunscreen, her nose was susceptible to sunburn. If I became concerned about the severity of her superficial injuries, I sought the opinion of our vet. To my relief, Dr. Goldy never found anything to support my fears.

Although our trips to the mountains were infrequent, Boo loved these escapes from the city and would scream with unbound excitement as evergreen breezes teased her senses. And there was always a chance we might come back with a good story or two.

The only other option was to explore the plains and expanding cities of the Rocky Mountain Front. It wasn't long before we discovered unique and remarkable wild places without leaving the metropolitan area.

For the past twenty years or so, ninety-nine percent of my time has been spent in southeast Denver and south Aurora. The place where I live, and where I raised Boo, looks like a typical suburban landscape with houses next to more houses that are connected by paved streets and regulated by stop signs, stoplights, and cone zones. Although the Rocky Mountains are visible from some locations, the horizon is mostly a staggered line of houses, apartments, office buildings, retail stores, and fringes of exotic shade trees.

And like other metropolitan areas, an ancient spirit has been buried beneath this urban sprawl. During my years as a dog person—and while looking for new places to explore—I have stumbled upon scattered prehistoric remnants within a fractured civilized veneer.

Denver and Aurora are located on the western side of the Colorado Piedmont. Although this geographic term is rarely used in the local dialect, it applies to a vast portion of the state. And most of this territory is a lonely expanse where tourism swells when someone misses the exit for the Denver International Airport. If I told any Coloradan I lived in the

Colorado Piedmont, they might express concern for my fanciful imagination. But if one shared my interest in trivia, she would envision the general area between Greeley and Pueblo.

When approaching Colorado from the east, the Great Plains climb into the High Plains and then gently crumple before resting against the foothills of the Rocky Mountains. This final transformation of the Great Plains, between the High Plains and the Rockies, is known as the Colorado Piedmont.

Unlike the High Plains to the east, which are more level, the Piedmont is composed of low rolling hills and rocky buttes. Small creeks, with or without flowing water, define the hills and buttes.

It's a land of geologic standing waves. There are very few trees in the Piedmont except crowds of cottonwoods and willows along the creek channels, and windbreaks around farms, ranches, and isolated developments. The pine trees that thrive in the western half of the state become a minority of isolated stands on elevated ridges. As this undulating and windswept landscape approaches the mountains, the dry grasslands are replaced by drive-through restaurants, shopping centers, public parks, and suburban communities. This is where golf carts assault the rolling hills during wasteful periods of recreation.

An inland sea covered much of Colorado until about seventy million years ago. The mountains were thousands of feet below a seabed of shale and sandstone. Then the Rockies sprouted upward within the ancient sea basin. Tropical lowlands satisfied the ponderous appetites of lumbering dinosaurs. Over time, cubic miles of sand and gravel flowed from the mountains and buried the eastern lowlands as well as valuable pockets of Cretaceous hydrocarbons. Volcanoes contributed flows of lava and ash. Creeks and streams arose upon this new plain and carved the sandstone and cobbles into lines of hills within the Piedmont.

The South Platte River, as it flows from the mountains and into the plains, is the matriarch of the northern Piedmont watershed. Effervescent mountain streams, which attract invasions of anglers and photographers, tumble down from the mountains and toward the South Platte. On the eastern side of this river, a series of modest creeks beg for moisture and recognition. When the original settlers established farms and ranches east of the South Platte, they struggled to create names for these trickles of water. Three of these were subsequently named First Creek, Second Creek, and Third Creek.

West of the South Platte River, the Piedmont has a slim presence. It's just a threshold for the real mountains. To the east, the Piedmont finds its true domain. And the city of Aurora is one of the gateways to this quiet and humble territory.

The anonymous hills and shallow valleys are largely composed of sand, silt, and clay. I verified this whenever it rained or snowed. On these occasions, the dogs and I returned home with samples on our feet. The clay is very aggressive and can increase my elevation by an inch or so as it accumulates beneath my boots.

Undeveloped patches of this rumpled plain can be found near my home. These are, as a rule, located around creeks and gulches where development is difficult and not recommended. Physically the Piedmont is still there but its soul is concealed within a superficial disguise.

Cherry Creek is the most notable watercourse that begins and ends within the Piedmont. It's also a Denver landmark and may have followed the same paleochannel (aka, stubborn routine) for millions of years. It begins at the Palmer Divide as a collection of several small tributaries. Unlike the Continental Divide, the Palmer Divide is a low and stumpy sandstone extension of the Rockies. It's also a boundary for several northern Piedmont aquifers. As Cherry Creek flows from this divide, it takes a northward trek toward Denver while gradually growing into a mighty—well, bigger—creek.

Within the city, Goldsmith Creek seeps from the ground and furtively flows through southeast Denver before joining Cherry Creek. Although this creek has been overwhelmed by progress, there are a few places like Rosamond Park, Bible Park, and Cook Park where it is allowed to be free and, sometimes, a little wild.

Just days before we became acquainted, Boo was lost and trying to survive along the banks of Goldsmith Creek in Bible Park.

KOKO

According to my records, Boo's story began with Koko.

My childhood days in Denver were shared with more than a few Siberian huskies. Except for my sister, Sara; a Scottish terrier; a poodle; and a Tigger; most of my siblings were huskies. My mom handled all doggy business and she settled on huskies as the perfect breed.

Nahni was my parents' last husky. She resembled a goofy red-haired clown, so my nickname for her was Bozo.

Toward the end of the 1990s, my mom went down to Dumb Friends to find a companion for Bozo. This animal shelter was not far from her home and, in the following years, would be the source of several new family members.

Mom was hoping to find another husky, but Dumb Friends was an unlikely place to find a purebred dog unless it had been orphaned, abandoned, or suffered some other unavoidable circumstance. I'm not saying Dumb Friends had bad dogs; they just had pets who had been denied refuge.

When Mom saw a miserable Shiba Inu named Koko, she knew she had found her dog.

The volunteers at Dumb Friends did their best to scuttle Mom's decision. Apparently Koko had smitten two previous owners with her charms. Each time she was returned to Dumb Friends after the honeymoon was over. If Koko failed to impress her owner one more time, this would have been her third strike—a dangerous trend toward incompatibility.

With her normal contrarian spirit, Mom was determined to adopt Koko and her conviction prevailed. Koko was finally welcomed into a home where the little devil dog would be obeyed for many years.

Around this time, I was absquatulating from Boise with a U-Haul trailer dragging behind my Camry. Although it was a rash decision, my uncertain future had spurred a quest for stability. Having no other plans or options, my only choice was to move to Denver and freeload on my parents until I could find a place of my own.

When I arrived at my mom and dad's house, I was greeted by thirty pounds of belligerence. Having expected a warm welcome, I was surprised by my parents' investment in an ankle-biting guard dog. This was my first encounter with a Shiba Inu. She resembled a miniature brown husky in appearance and a rattlesnake in attitude.

"Does it have a name?" I turned toward my folks as they welcomed me back.

"Grrrrrrr! A Rat! A Rat!"

"This is Koko!" My mom was beaming with pride.

"Grrrrrrr! A Rat! A Rat! A Rat! Grrrrrrrrr!"

I glanced over at the seething gatekeeper.

"Hmmmm. Oh, OK," I replied.

With awkward caution, I approached Koko with an offer of peaceful harmony. She raised her hackles high above her shoulders, displayed every tooth and fang with a fearsome snarl, and thwarted my diplomacy. Then Nahni pushed the arrogant brat aside and gave me some true love.

In fact, before Koko, all our family pets had been gentle souls. She introduced a new volatility. There was a standoff for a few days, maybe weeks, until Koko conceded to my annoying presence. Bozo's lovable influence may have mellowed Koko's aggression as well. As a demonstration of her growing acceptance, Koko claimed a portion of my bed. Each evening I would climb in beside her and run my hand along her soft fur until she bit me. That was her way of saying good night.

After a couple of months, I let Koko keep the bed and found a place of my own. But this was just the beginning of a fateful relationship.

Although a bond was growing between Koko and me, she was still my mom's dog. In Mom's opinion, Dumb Friends had misjudged her dog's character. And to prove this fact, her goal was to train Koko to be an exceptional obedience and agility champion.

Anyone who is familiar with the dog sport of agility envisions dogs flying over jumps, racing across elevated planks, rocketing through tunnels, and whipping around weave poles. This wasn't Koko. In her mind, agility was a thoughtfully savored and leisurely paced activity.

I attended my first agility trial to provide moral support for my mom. My usefulness also extended to hauling her gear down to a day-camping site near the agility courses.

Mom's camping necessities included a large shade tent, a wall-to-wall floor mat, a crate with a plush mattress for Koko, two battery-powered fans, collapsible chairs, a cooler with food and beverages, and a bag of doggy supplies. A small transistor radio tuned to KVOD created an air of refinement. With the addition of a hand-truck and a pull-cart, which were necessary to transport everything, this was our standard agility gear. We would not be roughing it.

It was a fine summer day on the playing fields at Jefferson County Fairgrounds. My mom and Koko had been attending agility classes for about four months, and this was the second or third time they had competed in an official trial. As I watched Mom and the uncompromising varmint run through the courses, I was quite impressed.

Unfortunately, the thrill of actual competition lasted

only a few minutes. The remaining hours were filled with not much. For most of the day, while my mom was absent from our tent and assisting with various agility trial duties, Koko and I whittled away the doldrums at our campsite. Like other four-legged competitors around us, she was confined to her crate and less than happy with this arrangement.

When empathy overruled my common sense, I decided to free the poor girl from her cruel confinement. I believed this act of kindness would be rewarded with thankful obedience. After unlatching Koko's crate and opening the door, life sprang back into her pitiful expression.

It was bad timing. Her attention immediately shifted toward the bug-screen side of the tent where a competitor and her dog were passing by. Two seconds later, the screen was shredded and the angry woman and willful Shiba began sharing pleasantries. Satisfied with her efforts, Koko took a hard left and disappeared into the mass of people, dogs, and tents.

A terrified chorus of "Loose dog! Loose dog!" identified the path of her escape. My pursuit ended at the picnic shelter where Mom was organizing scores and ribbons for the competitors. At her side was a perfect Shiba angel. Koko's actions were beyond reproach. And the fact that I had been deceived fell on deaf ears.

About a year later, Mom had a minor stroke. Everybody was worried—except Mom. She was more concerned about Koko's future as an indisputable champion. To fulfill Koko's destiny, the weekly agility class became my job. I survived an awkward doggy sports learning curve and found a strange satisfaction in jogging around agility courses while shouting hopeful commands to a headstrong dog.

While attending training classes or official trials—and

not conquering the agility courses—Koko was kept on a short leash or inside her crate. During these interludes, she became a vigilant defender of the space around us. Any dog who crossed her invisible boundary was greeted with a light snarl and suggestive display of teeth and gums.

There was not much sympathy for aggressive behavior within the dog sports community. Most of the contestants were well-mannered and respectful of each other. This was an unofficial law among the competitors. When up to a hundred or more pups coexisted within a limited amount of space, canine athletes with bossy attitudes were not welcome. All the same, my mom and I proudly defended our position at the bottom of the agility popularity contest. And we were never tempted to break Koko's fiery spirit.

Prior to competing, the human handlers and their furry partners would line up near the course entrance and wait for their turn. A sense of order was maintained by having each dog restrained with a leash. This proximity to a gaggle of tail-wagging dunces always annoyed Koko. To keep her calm, I would lay on top of her, with her grumbling nose exposed below my arm. It was like lying on a shrunken bear rug that was still alive.

One time, while I was pinning Koko to the ground near the start of the course, two elderly harpies came over and hovered above our bodies. Then they offered some advice. According to their ancient wisdom, Koko should not have been competing in agility.

"That dog does not belong here!" Snarkwelda snorted.

"Yes! Its temperament is horrible!" Snootina huffed.

"Grrrrrrr. Ahrrrrrrrr," Koko responded.

"Thanks," I added.

With these words of encouragement, we completed a

near-perfect run. Another woman near the finish line congratulated us and said, "Now you can tell those old hags to go fuck themselves." This was so sweet.

Astonishingly, whenever I freed Koko from her leash and told her to wait before the first obstacle, she would ignore the other dogs and patiently wait until I gave her the signal to go. Perhaps she knew it was time to put her trash talk aside and become a focused, albeit slow, athlete. She really tried and we had many proud moments. Maybe Mom was right. Maybe she could be a champion.

I still remember the day when Koko earned her Open Agility title. This was a historic achievement, so I called my mom and covered every detail of the qualifying run like a proud daddy.

The bond between Koko and me grew stronger every day. When she lounged next to me on the sofa, she squatted on her hind legs and leaned back. It was uncanny how this upright pose resembled a lazy baboon on a *National Geographic* documentary. So she became the Monkey Girl. She may have preferred something more respectable like Queen of Shiba, but I liked Monkey Girl.

PINKIE

It wasn't long before Mom's health returned to full capacity. Then she wanted her dog back. Even though Koko had not deserted her, Mom was aware of her dog's shifting alliances. It was time to find another dog for me.

One day, she called me at work. "I've found a beautiful Aussie at Dumb Friends!"

"An Aussie?"

I knew what an Australian shepherd was, but like I said, you usually don't find purebreds at Dumb Friends. And I could see where this was heading.

"She's beautiful! You will love her! Other people were also looking at her, so I paid the down payment."

"Oh boy. OK. How old?"

I'm terrible with commitments. Adopting a dog was not part of my life plans at that moment.

"They think she's about one year old. They found her in Bible Park with no identification."

"Does she have a name?"

"They call her Pinkie."

The Dumb Friends' web page included pictures of their homeless pets who were up for adoption. Each portrait showed an animal with a large nose and small head facing the camera. When I went to their website, I found a Pinkie with a huge pink nose on a tiny black-and-white face. It was an awful caricature. I wish I had saved a copy for posterity.

This happened on Friday, May 23, 2003. On Saturday, my mom and I drove to Dumb Friends to see Pinkie. Koko joined us as well. Although her approval was unlikely, her opinion would be noted in my deliberations.

Soon after arriving, we were escorted to an empty visiting room with a concrete shelf that served as a bench. The accommodations were somber and sterile. Howls and barks of other dogs echoed outside the door. Koko's displeasure was quite evident. Her memories of Dumb Friends may have been filled with dark uncertainty.

When Pinkie was brought into the room, she carried herself with delicate strength. Her light steps barely touched the floor as she kept a safe distance. Although her coat was full, it was short for an Aussie and highlighted her sinuous muscles. And she was almost completely white except for a black ear, black eye patch, and black bobbed tail.

She was built like a miniature racehorse. Like a vessel designed to contain a strong spirit. Simply beautiful. I had found my dog.

I found her hiding behind my legs and beneath the concrete bench where she was seeking protection from an offended Shiba who was sporting a wrinkled nose. After admonishing Koko, I sat down on the floor, held my hand beneath Pinkie's nose, and then, for the first time, felt her silky coat.

Was I ready for this? No. Had I made my decision? Yes.

Two days after this visit, on Memorial Day, Pinkie had been spayed and was ready to join me on our first adventure. To celebrate this fateful transition, Dumb Friends tied a beautiful scarf around her neck. It was a swirling blend of deep-blue and aqua-blue with images of stars, frosted fir trees, and flying angels. The angels almost looked like fairies, but to a discerning eye, they were obviously angels.

The scarf was a frail, but lovely, adornment. As it could not be used to control Pinkie, I was given an inexpensive leash that slipped over her head and around her neck.

With a firm, yet nervous grip, I led her into the parking lot. Rain was falling and the sky grew darker. Suddenly, a bolt of lightning struck nearby and a bolt of adrenalin shot through Pinkie's veins. She nearly pulled the leash out of my hand, but I tightened my grip as the plastic rope cinched around her neck. When I opened the door to my truck, Pinkie's anxiety led to resistance. I did my best to calm her down. At this point, I was immune to the drenching downpour. Taking her wet and trembling body into my arms, I lifted her into my cab. Then I got in, looked over at the frightened girl, and saw the beginning of another chapter in my life.

I've often wondered about her memories of this day. Pinkie was groggy from general anesthesia and heading into a new life in a foreign world. And she was stuck with a guy who had never raised a dog.

They say raising a dog is easier than raising a child. I don't know about children—never been there. But it was a significant effort to raise a young dog who could vanish in an instant, destroy a leash with little effort, and fly over barriers that would cripple most humans. The unsavory things that found their way into her mouth will not be mentioned. At the same time, it was not necessary to toilet train my new companion; she knew how to take care of this. In fact, her natural maturity forced me to adapt faster than I had anticipated.

The first baby step was to give her a real name. As she was an Aussie and I was a *Crocodile Hunter* fan, my choice was obvious. I named her Sheila. This was awkward when I began working with a woman who had the same name. Over time, as I will explain, this name did not stick.

But for now, she was my beautiful little Sheila.

SHEILA

Sheila was perfectly suited to become a great agility dog. She was intelligent, fast, obedient, and, of course, agile. While attending trials with Koko, I had watched other Aussies race through the courses with mad enthusiasm. Koko thought their behavior was a bit excessive. The Monkey Girl had no appetite for haste unless there was a bunny on the other end.

While Sheila was still in training, Koko was competing in American Kennel Club (AKC) trials. If Sheila were to compete in AKC as well, a small bureaucratic issue had to be resolved. AKC only allowed purebreds or Indefinite Listing Privilege (ILP) dogs to compete. An ILP dog was one who resembled a purebred but lacked official documentation that confirmed its lineage.

Koko was registered as an ILP Shiba Inu. Like Koko, Sheila had no record of her past. Competing in AKC would not be possible unless we passed the ILP approval process.

To prove Sheila was a purebred Australian shepherd, I prepared an AKC application with a photo of my girl and a description of her behavior. If they agreed with my assessment and believed Sheila was not a mixed-breed mutt, she would then receive their blessing as an ILP Aussie.

Her ear set was perfect and appropriately drooped, so the photo was easy. To capture the essence of her spirit, I bought a book called *The Essential Australian Shepherd* and transcribed the ideal traits. Then I created a fictitious birth date (11/19/2001) and mailed the information to AKC.

For several months, I waited for their response and suspected my plagiarism and fiction had been discovered. This wouldn't have been the end of the world. There were other options for competing in agility. Then I received a letter from a man in Kent, Washington:

November 8, 2003

Dear Mr. Frisbie,

I mistakenly received the enclosed AKC ILP for your Sheila. It was inadvertently included with the forms for my dog. I certainly hope this delay hasn't caused you to miss any tests or events.

⹁ John

Yes! Thanks to this considerate man (as well as AKC's honorable opinion), I could officially fantasize about future AKC agility achievements with Sheila running by my side.

And no, we hadn't missed any tests or events; we were still struggling through obedience classes and some simple agility training.

An agility dog should also be an obedient dog. Not as a pet, but as an accomplice. A partnership should be nourished with rewards and praise. Rather than creating a useful animal, it's more like inviting a furry kindred spirit into a crazy endeavor.

Koko excelled at obedience. That's not a joke—it's a fact. She and Mom would earn several AKC obedience titles. But for Koko, compliance worked both ways, and she always demanded submission from any man or beast who came within her sphere of influence.

To say obedience training was fun would be a stretch. In fact, it was tedious when compared to agility training. For a couple of months, once per week, Sheila and I drove to Kiowa for doggy school. In the end, we survived and received a certificate for completing beginner's obedience. That was enough for me and we turned our focus onto agility.

Agility demanded intensive training as well. Progress was achieved with hours of drills and piles of treats. The name "Sheila," which was applied before or after commands, was beginning to lose its luster. All the same, I was working with a true athlete and it was an exciting and captivating period of my life.

Around this time, my agility trainer, Mary Beth, became suspicious of my girl's appearance. According to her, Sheila appeared to be a "lethal white" and may have a short life. She was a what? How long would she live? Boo was an unusual Aussie, but her health was above normal. This phrase didn't reflect the vitality she possessed. My research into this topic led to myriad conclusions and disturbing high school memories.

Lethal white is a genetic trait that is similar to albinism. Although some might argue with this claim, I'm trying to simplify a complex biological blueprint.

Maybe I'm diving too deep into the weeds, but I must dredge out those old biology lectures about fruit flies and dominant and recessive genes. Remember those big words that filled the overhead projector screen: homozygous and heterozygous? For me this invokes reoccurring nightmares where I stumble into the final exam without studying or getting dressed. As I proceed into this discussion, please just play along and thank me for not mentioning quadratic equations.

These terrifying terms are important for describing the lethal white trait. While this condition occurs within many breeds of dogs and other animals, it's quite common in Australian shepherds. Some Aussies have handsome mottled-colored coats and are called "merles." Their appearance is often expressed through heterozygous ingredients. Merles are great pets and stockdogs, but their genetics can lead to risky breeding. Although breeders are extremely careful about not mating two merle Aussies, it sometimes happens. When merles are allowed to breed with each other, some of the puppies (depending on the size of the litter) may have harmful homozygous traits. These pups are easily identified by their predominant whiteness.

Some folks call them "double merles." While this is technically correct, it can be misleading. The white puppies might be culled from the litter. Ultimately this may require a lethal solution.

Even though this trait is not necessarily lethal, the lack of pigmentation may cause deafness. Impaired vision is a risk as well. I have seen healthy adult lethal whites with various degrees of deafness or blindness, and my heart goes out to their owners. One Aussie whom I always recognize at the dog park is named Lily. Lily is completely white and deaf. Although she was born with a total lack of pigmentation, her physical appearance and spirit remind me of Sheila. And like Sheila, her pink nose has gradually blackened over the years.

In a perfect world, there would be no Lily. And the greatest companion I've ever known would have never been born. And even though I discourage the siring of lethal whites, without her imperfections Sheila would not have been Sheila.

Despite having two eyes with different colors, Sheila's vision was quite good. She had a brown eye on the white side of her face, and a white eye on the black side.

Her ears were a different story. One ear was black (with a white albatross silhouette) and the other was white. While the black ear functioned as expected, the white ear was only a prop. Therefore she could detect sounds but couldn't determine their source. And she could disable her good ear and ignore my words of wisdom.

Although Sheila's coat was almost completely white, her pink skin was mottled with patches of grey. This was noticeable on her belly and whenever the vet shaved other parts of her body. This suggested she had a good dollop of heterozygosity, along with a full whack of other complex attributes.

She was perfectly healthy, but I still worried.

CHASING THE DREAM

PART ONE

Sheila was a fast learner. After four months of training, we were ready to test her skills in actual competitions. My job, as her handler, was to briskly recite a litany of commands while spinning and dodging through an array of jumps, tunnels, and whatever. Although to a lesser degree, agility was also required for handlers.

We were a team. A very small team. The glory of success was shared between us. Any failure was my responsibility.

It was dialog of physical and verbal cues. A slight twist of my hips or shoulders were as effective as a loud command. I taught her "left" meant turn left, "right" meant turn right, and "go go go" meant just that. These skills were a source of amusement if I confused my left and right—and my girl always did as she was told.

At the start of each course, I told Sheila to sit and wait. Then I'd walk beyond the first obstacle and tell her to go. From there, if our stars were aligned, it went something like this:

Jump! Go! Jump! Go! Jump! Yarph! Left! Climb! Urr, yarph! Yarph! Easy. Easy. (I'm using a front cross to control her). Touch. Touch. Good girl! Right! Yarph! Big! Right! Walk! Easy. Easy. (Again, using a front cross). Urr, urr, yarph! Touch. Touch. Good girl! Left! Go! Jump! Out! Weave! Weave weave weave weave weave weave. (I take a quick breath). Weave weave weave weave weave weave. Yarph! Yarph! Good Girl! Go! Big! Go! Jump! Here! Chute! Go! Jump! Right! Yarph! Jump! (I stay back to pull her into the tunnel). Go!

Tunnel! Left, left! (I'm letting her know how to exit the tunnel.) Here! Table! Down! Good girl. Stay. Stay. Stay. Stay. Go! Tire! Yarph! Left! Jump! Here! Jump! (I use a front cross to guide her to the see-saw.) Here! Teeter! Easy. Easy. Yarph! Yarph! Touch. Touch. Good girl! Go! Yarph! Big! Go! Yay! (I jump up and down and clap my hands like a little boy.)

The experience became more humbling as we advanced into higher levels of competition. At a trial in Pueblo, one of the best teams in the world showed us how to do it properly. In contrast to my frenetic style, Marcus Topps and Juice ran in near-silence as they tore through the course. Their communication and coordination were so subtle, they might have been a single organism. It's teams like this that elevate the respect for this sport.

PART TWO

The demographics of the human competitors leaned heavily toward the female tribe. At the same time, men were encouraged to attend the events and manhandle vast piles of hardware that were required for a competition. To resolve this critical conundrum, women would drag their husbands and boyfriends to the event, promise them free food, and put them to work.

A handful of men, like me, accepted the challenge of these doggy circuses. It's likely each of us had unwittingly stumbled upon this sport before becoming trapped within its crazy addiction.

In addition to AKC, Boo and I began competing with other agility organizations that had long names and short abbreviations. These included the United States Dog Agility Association (USDAA) and the North American Dog Agility

Council (NADAC, pronounced "nay-dak"). USDAA was for serious athletes. Sheila had to clear twenty-two-inch jumps in these trials, rather than the twenty-inch jumps that were preferred by AKC and NADAC.

Both USDAA and NADAC were supporters of the common mutt and allowed any dog of known or unknown breeding to compete.

Sheila also competed in trials that were sponsored by the Australian Shepherd Club of America (ASCA, or "aska"). The ASCA trials were often co-sponsored by NADAC, and any qualifying points were tallied by both organizations.

Yes, it was all about the qualifying points. Similar to counting coup, these measured success or failure at the end of each day. Points led to titles and titles led to more points and more titles. Folks would travel the entire country and spend each weekend at various agility venues while increasing their stature with points, titles, ribbons, trophies, and Homeric achievements.

My mom and Koko often joined us at AKC and NADAC competitions. NADAC was perfect for folks who preferred to have fun rather than achieve doggy immortality. These trials were ideal for Koko's reserved competitive spirit.

In AKC events, the dogs wore collars during their runs. In USDAA and NADAC, the dogs ran naked (in other words, without collars). The human handlers were always required to be appropriately dressed.

In addition to "standard" and "jumpers" courses, which were the core of any agility trial, USDAA and NADAC included a variety of "games," such as gamblers, snooker, and relays.

In standard and jumpers courses, each team completed the jumps and other obstacles in a specific order, and results were based on time and faults. The faults were always the handler's fault. Gamblers and snooker demanded a greater level of handling skill.

At the beginning of a gamblers run, each team could select any obstacle, improve their score, and keep doing this until time expired. All competitors were allotted the same amount of time for this part of the run. Then they faced the gamble—a series of obstacles that had to be completed in a specific order. The gamble was isolated from the rest of the course with a line of surveyor's tape that was laid across the ground. The handlers were forbidden from going beyond this boundary. Only dogs could enter the area where the gamble had been placed. It was like piloting a dog by remote control. In other words, with frantic screaming and waving, the handler guided his teammate through the gamble.

Snooker tested the athletes' ability to complete an obstacle, avoid any number of other obstacles, then repeat this confusion until they ran out of time. Historically, this contest inspired the construction of roadway roundabouts where stop signs would have been sufficient.

Relays were exciting, amusing, and nerve-racking. There were two types of "teams" and to avoid confusion, the dog and handler team was called a "pair." Two pairs made a relay "team." One pair ran the first half of the course and the other tackled the second half. As one might guess, holding and exchanging the baton was awkward, and sometimes it was mistaken for a dog toy.

PART THREE

A regiment of volunteers was the heart and soul of a successful event. This labor force was composed of handlers, friends, and family members who had a common desire to be useful. Judging the competition was the only non-volunteer task. This job was handled by judges who were shipped in from distant jurisdictions and compensated for their draconian expertise.

Each agility course was enclosed within a rectangular area known as the "ring". "Corral" would be more accurate, but ring was simpler. And the dimensions had to be perfect.

For building a course, the judge would provide a detailed copy of her design to the chief course-setter. Armed with a spool of measuring tape for longitude and his trusty measuring wheel for latitude, the chief course-setter and a small legion of volunteers would then arrange the actual obstacles. Tolerances could be less than six inches.

After the volunteers had constructed the course, the judge assumed primacy and would review the accuracy of their efforts. This assessment included pensively strolling through the course while squinting, scowling, measuring distances with precise strides, rearranging obstacles, and, ultimately, nodding with approval. During this process, she might modify the course despite the volunteers' precise replication of the official version. Indeed, judges often forgot to include the curvature of the earth in their initial designs.

Only the handlers could study the course. The dogs were oblivious to what they were about to face. There were no practice runs. And this was why it was inhumane to blame a pup for any mishaps.

With the course-setters relieved of their duty, the judge would turn toward the waiting competitors and address them with a resonant bellow, "The course is now open for inspection!" or something to that effect. Then the handlers would spill into the ring and perform an odd, improvised ballet as they prepared for their run.

While studying standard and jumpers courses, the handlers would form an interweaving conga line. And while rehearsing individual strategies for gamblers and snooker, the risk for collisions from asynchronous choreography was often palpable. Watching these avant-garde dancers and their imaginary pets was always entertaining.

Then it was time to free our pups and face the challenge.

As they raced through the agility course, the dogs had to accept the presence of a strange person who would gesture and shadow them for the entire run. This, once again, was the scrupulous judge asserting her authority and noting any merits or demerits that were accumulated by each team.

For almost four years, we devoted most of our weekends to this obsession. Koko filed her retirement papers after two years. As I forged ahead with Sheila, her passion gradually waned despite my efforts to rekindle her competitive fire. This was understandable. She was mostly confined inside her crate while I diverted my energy into a variety of volunteer activities.

To maintain a sense of normalcy, the girls and I would leave the venue to stretch our legs and delineate our territory. Finding a swimming hole was critical on hot days. Trials were commonly held at fairgrounds or parks where open spaces, ponds, and creeks provided these creature comforts. On one of these excursions, Koko and Sheila teamed up and bagged a rabbit near the agility courses. The Monkey Girl wanted to keep it as a present for the harpies, but this was not going to happen.

BOO-BOO

Yes, Sheila was given a funny and awkward name. I still love this name and it suited her quite well. Her veterinary records listed her as Sheila Frisbie and this gave me some paternal satisfaction. Her official agility title was Frisbie's Sheila and I called her Sheila for most of her agility career.

Which brings us to the popular question: what's in a name? It depends on the perspective. It might be an ageless summary of an exceptional life and accomplishments. Or maybe it's a bookmark for a friend or associate.

Koko will always be Koko. Nahni will always be Nahni. These names embrace the whole of their lives.

And Sheila will always be Sheila.

Then there's the spirit. Many times the spirit name assumes the given name and sometimes it doesn't. Naming Sheila's spirit was not deliberate. It was an accidental process and I wish I could say I just changed her name.

Like other athletic pursuits, agility came with a physical toll. Sheila often attacked the courses with reckless zeal. Although she could clear a jump by six inches, sometimes she got distracted and took out an entire triple jump. Training and trials took place over a variety of surfaces ranging from concrete to grassy playing fields. Hard surfaces resulted in abrupt landings and minor shoulder injuries. Deep grass made clearing jumps more difficult. Her knuckles and forelegs often felt the sting of the PVC pipe crossbars.

Near the end of our agility days, I totaled my truck while driving to the second day of an event in Castle Rock. A snowstorm had blanketed southbound I-25 and I cautiously selected the middle lane. The car in front of us lost control, rotated ninety degrees, and came to a stop. Sheila was beside me on the passenger side. This was her preferred seat and had never been an issue.

I reached over with my right arm and tried to pin Sheila to her seat. An instant later, we went straight into the driver's side of the other car. The slick road buffered the impact and the other driver was not injured.

After the accident, I looked over to see if Sheila was OK. Even though her entire body was trembling, there were no apparent injuries. A large spiderweb crack in the windshield on her side prevented me from ignoring how bad it could have been.

I blamed myself for exposing her to this risk. The front seat of a car is not a safe place for a pet. The passenger-side airbag had been disabled and this was my only credit for precaution. But Sheila never displayed any trauma after the collision and continued to ride beside me throughout the following years.

Later that day, I borrowed Mom's car to retrieve my gear at the agility event. As a consolation for our misfortune, a photographer gave me a photo of Sheila ripping through the weave poles. This picture had been taken on the previous day and vividly captured my girl's focus and spirit. I have a stack of agility photos and this one stands out. It reminds me of this terrible day and the kind people who tried to make it better. And it reminds me of Sheila's rock-solid resilience.

Whether it was recklessness, debatable care, or bad karma, Sheila was prone to injury. This started with Koko leaving a small gash on Sheila's pink nose. The Monkey Girl was rankled by this new dog, but over time, her irritation diminished until growing into a strong kinship with her affectionate alter ego.

Then there was the grass seed in my girl's ear. This caused unbearable discomfort and resulted in a veterinary bill for about two hundred dollars. And then she stuck her nose in a yellow jacket nest and acquired a bulbous snout for a day or so. And the dings just kept coming.

Tile floors and reckless energy don't mix. This resulted in a list of minor dings.

As a young girl, Sheila was often the target of other dogs as they chased her around the dog park. To evade them, she would crash, tumble, and bounce to her feet after the pack had passed by. Although this was impressive, she must have been covered with bruises beneath her white coat.

Her contempt for coyotes didn't help either. Back when she was abandoned or lost in Bible Park, and before she was found and taken to Dumb Friends, her life was probably filled with coyote confrontations. A single molecule of coyote scent made her hackles stand straight up from nose to tail. Then her head swung back and forth as she tasted the air to confirm the origin of the stink. And it wasn't a growl or bark, but a furious scream that prefaced her intentions.

We avoided serious conflicts for over two years until a coyote-tinged miasma drifted from a heavily vegetated swale during our morning walk. Sheila's irritation spread to her vocal cords and every follicle along her back. Clearing her mind of thoughtfulness and caution, she chased the invisible trail into the swampy thicket. Within seconds, a riot of shrieks and screams erupted from the swamp. Before I had any time to digest the sequence of events, she was back by my side and seemed to be OK, so we continued down the trail.

When we reached the edge of a nearby pond, I tossed a

stick into the water. This was my girl's traditional morning bath. Instead of leaping into the pond, she slowly entered the water and began to yelp in pain as the water came over her back. When she exited the pond, I saw blood streaming down her flanks. The coyote battle had been more violent than I had suspected and she had received several deep wounds. Somehow her dry fur had concealed the bleeding. When her fur became wet, the degree of her injury was quite apparent.

Her brief conflict must have involved an organized attack by several coyotes. It's a common coyote tactic where one holds the dog's attention while others move in from behind.

This incident occurred during the early years of our steady relationship with the Goldsmith Veterinary Clinic. After the vets had shaved, cleaned, and stitched several boo-boos, the mottled pink-and-grey skin on her backside was laced with angry red sutures.

Throughout this period of her life, I commonly used the phrase, "You are such a boo-boo." Over time, this was shortened to "Boo-boo" and soon became my new name for her. Eventually, as a matter of efficiency, her name simply became Boo.

Whenever her old name was used, she knew she had been a naughty girl. And to avoid confusion, the credentials that hung from her collar always identified her as Sheila.

Before she was Pinkie, Sheila, or Boo, she had another name that may reside in someone's memory. Don't ask me how I know, but it must have been Angel. Many of our friends will doubt my clairvoyance.

For the rest of her days, she would be Boo. Some folks assumed this name came from her ghost-like appearance. This worked for me as well.

THE PACK

Cities are made for humans. Whenever we need to be there, get this, or do that, it's probably a short drive away. Once in a while, if it doesn't interfere with commerce or convenience, a small patch of open land is spared.

At the same time, the Denver area has an influential canine constituency and may have the best dog parks in America. Over the years, these have become more regulated and crowded, but they are still great for unwinding and sniffing butts.

Cherry Creek State Park has everything a city dog would desire. And it's only a few miles from my home. Both a state park pass and a dog park pass are required to visit the Cherry Creek dog park. To assist my finances, my mom would purchase two senior citizen passes—one for her and one for me. They looked exactly like non-senior citizen passes. This discount lasted until the state began issuing only one pass per vehicle.

The state park has two areas where dogs can run freely: the dog park where it is legal, and the rest of the park where pets must be tethered to their owners before wandering along officially established paths. When we explored beyond the dog park boundaries, we followed the established trails as a brief convenience then spent the rest of our time following deer trails and instinct. As a precaution, two six-foot leashes fit perfectly inside my back pocket.

*savage \ săv'ĭj \ adj. **1.** Untouched by man and civilization; not domesticated or cultivated; wild. **2.** Not civilized; primitive; barbaric. **3.** Ferocious; fierce. **4.** Vicious or* *merciless; brutal. **5**. Lacking in polish or manners; rude —n. **1**. A primitive or uncivilized person. **2**. A brutal, fierce, or vicious people. **3**. A rude person; a boor. —tr. v. **savaged, -aging, -ages**. **1**. To attack violently. **2**. To make angry or fierce. **3**. To bite or trample ferociously. [Middle English* sauvage, *from Old French, from Common Romance* salvãticus *(unattested), from Latin* silvãticus, *of the woods, wild, from* silva, *woods, forest. See* **sylvan**.*]

So stated *The American Heritage Dictionary of The English Language* forty-six years ago. I assume the definition hasn't changed since then. Did such a word exist prior to civilization? The boorish and uncultivated barbarians must have used a similar demeaning term. Indeed, it may go back to a deeper origin: of the woods or forest. Having read too many *Tarzan* books as a child, I prefer a more elevated meaning. And a few words below "savage" one will find "savant"—just a coincidence?

Can a man walk out of the woods and leave his savagery behind? Can millions of years of adaptation be removed from his soul? Are the roots of culture deep or shallow?

Dogs are even more closely connected to their savage past. Even though Boo was an extremely civil dog, and seemed to possess a sense of empathy, her feral nature often prevailed. As for Koko, she was an unfiltered progression of a wise and tenacious ancestry.

Before I met Koko, I was an upstanding and model citizen. Then, thanks to her rebellious influence, I devolved into a compulsive law-breaking sociopath. Half of my life had been wasted by trying to be Mr. Nice Guy. Now I could push the limits of my delinquency.

Shibas are known as "runners" because they have a

reputation for taking off and disappearing. In this sense, the Monkey Girl was not a runner. Sure, she would dash away and chase bunnies and deer, but she always came back. I only lost her once. As I ran around and screamed her name, a man calmly walked up to me and described a dog who resembled Koko. He said she was waiting back by my car.

Another demonstration of her reliability (and impulsive behavior) occurred when she and my mom were driving home after a few hours of shopping. Koko was in the back seat and studying the scenery that rolled past her open window. Then something by the road piqued Koko's curiosity. Whatever it was, a closer inspection was necessary. I assume my mom was at a stoplight or something similar. Mom was unaware her car was thirty-five pounds lighter until she got home. After retracing her route, she found the Monkey Girl sitting on the side of the road where, presumably, she had jumped out.

Koko, Boo, and I visited every untamed Front Range area that we could find. These included a few dog parks as well as various pockets of undeveloped land. The dog parks at Cherry Creek and Chatfield were not fenced-in for many years. This exposed a significant amount of acreage for exploring, getting lost, and discovering things to chase. We knew every wild inch of these places.

Koko and Boo quickly joined forces and formed a small but effective dog pack. Each girl had her own unique set of attributes and their individual talents coalesced into a hunting machine.

Even though Boo was a passionate hunter, she lacked the ferocity for completing this task. One morning, she walked up to me with a live baby rabbit stuffed inside her mouth. It looked like she had been infected by an alien furry-tongue disease. When I freed the little guy from her jaws, its only injury was a healthy coating of saliva. Another time, she excavated a bunny nest, removed the babies, dug another hole, filled it with unharmed baby rabbits, and covered them with dirt. I tried to fix this situation, but I'm not sure if I saved them.

When pursuing rabbits, she often wedged herself into tight spaces like culverts and beneath storage sheds. If Boo had become stuck in any of these bunny condos, her rescue might have required the use of heavy equipment. But this was never necessary. She just threw her butt into reverse and, inch by inch, wiggled back into daylight.

Koko was a predator. It's likely all Shibas are natural mousers. If she detected a slight smell or rustling in the weeds, her attack was completed in less than one second—as if her sinews were forged from spring steel. Then her job was done. She had no appetite for her victims. Before Boo came into our lives, Nahni was always grateful for the free snack. But Boo had the same appetite for mice that Koko had.

Whenever Koko caught a rabbit, it became a trophy that dangled from her mouth until I could find a means of disposal (neither of us had a small-game license). Popular game birds were also on her shopping list, and she nearly added a brace of pheasants to her criminal record. I had several strategies to cover this possibility. Each contingency included a gourmet French or Asian recipe. Unfortunately, although she tried, she only caught their scent as they flew away.

It was Boo's terrifying shriek that Koko valued. This fearsome noise inspired squirrels and bunnies to flee straight toward Koko's jaws.

I fully understood how this scream could have a suicidal effect upon squirrels and rabbits. As my copilot, Boo assumed the task of screaming at every coyote, deer, or cow that lounged by the road. During these tirades, I often experienced extreme pain while my cranium vibrated at high frequencies. If you've ever held an electric guitar too close to a Fender Twin amplifier, it was a similar sensation. Over time, I learned to keep my earplugs within reach whenever we drove through places that could set her off. The only loud noise that didn't offend her was her own voice.

Chasing deer was a fun but wasted effort and the girls eventually abandoned their big-game pursuits. They didn't chase horses either. There were days when folks from a nearby stable would ride their ponies through the Cherry Creek dog park—I can't explain their reasoning. While the girls showed no aggression as the riders passed by, both had the annoying habit of wandering over to get a nose-full of horse aroma. To control this impulse, physical restraint was often necessary. The scent of the horses might have reminded them of a tasty treat known as road apples.

When it came to handling coyotes, Boo usually took the lead. Koko didn't mind using caution. Sometimes their wires got crossed.

A good example of bad coordination was demonstrated along a cattail swamp at the Cherry Creek dog park. Two coyotes appeared as they trotted toward the swamp. Before assessing her intent, Koko chased after them. She never made a sound while pursuing other animals—she was a child of the woods not sportscaster. Boo should have been at her side or in the lead but, instead, her nose was glued to the ground beneath the tall ryegrass.

Then the coyotes stopped at the edge of the cattails and turned around. The Monkey Girl also paused, noticed Boo was missing, and expressed concern. She needed help.

"Boo! Kyo!" By this time the reference had almost been reduced to a single syllable. It was as effective as hitting her on the butt with a hard slap.

Koko relaxed and sat down when the screaming white demon flew by her and pursued the coyotes into the swamp. Her sensibility had returned and she had no reason to follow Boo into the thick cattails. I agreed with the Monkey Girl's wisdom, so both of us waited and followed Boo's play-by-play coverage of the action. A minute or so later, the black-legged Aussie emerged from the cattails with her tongue dangling from a wide grin.

Boo and Koko's pack never included me. Membership in a dog pack requires a level of physical worthiness, and slow runners are categorically excluded. All the same, Boo and I shared a pack-like relationship when we were on our own.

The golf course in our neighborhood was littered with rabbits. At night, gangs of bunnies foraged in the middle of the fairways. When Boo was young and wild, her urge to chase after them was controlled by my firm grip on the leash. I feared she might chase a bunny into the surrounding streets. As she matured and became a better listener, I allowed her to run free and harass the crowds of cottontails. Soon I became a willing participant in her bunny quests.

After telling Boo to sit and stay on one side of a pack of rabbits, I'd walk around to the other side. At this point, she was ready to explode, but I'd remind Boo of her job and test her patience. This was like putting mega-torque on a rubber-band toy. When I finally gave the signal, she became a big fuzzy cue ball with bunnies scattering in all directions. If bunny-busting were a real sport, we would have been state champions.

FIRST VACATION

PART ONE

Three months after Boo's adoption, I was preparing for my annual camping trip. This time my buddies from Idaho, Tim and Darrin, would be joining me on the western side of the Big Hole Valley in Montana.

Spending a few days exploring the backcountry as well as long nights around the campfire were only part of this vacation. The second part would be attending a wedding in southwest Idaho.

My initial plan was to leave Boo with my mom and dad. Her shaved belly still betrayed her pre-adoption surgery. The intangible risks of camping in the wilds of Montana weighed heavily on my decision. It was a last-minute decision to take Boo along with me. Her loyalty and reliability tipped the scales. It seemed as if we had shared a much longer time together. My days of traveling in solitude were over. While packing camping supplies into my truck, I grabbed a colorful beach bag, which was a beautiful present from my sister, and filled this with Boo's doggy supplies and food. Then we hit the road.

During our first three months together, our longest car ride had lasted about fifteen minutes. The trip to Montana would be nine hours on the first day as we traveled across Wyoming. The second day would demand another six hours on the road.

My strategy was to let Boo stretch her legs and claim a patch of grass whenever I needed gas or a break for myself. In Laramie, Boo got out of the truck and sniffed around. Then she sniffed and sniffed some more and had no urge to do anything else. There was no other business on her agenda. This was the same story at the Fort Steele rest stop, followed by the same story in Rawlins and Lander.

Meanwhile, between stops, she rarely sat still. She would stand on her seat, sit down for a brief period, lay her head on my knee for fifteen seconds, return to standing on her seat, then repeat this routine many, many times. It was not unreasonable to assume her bladder was about to explode.

This long and restless drive finally brought us to a campsite west of Dubois, Wyoming near Union Pass. I shut off my engine and we became immersed in the primal forest solitude that always haunts my city sensibilities. A mountain stream flowing by our camp tickled the silence. Conifers and sagebrush filled the waning daylight with a light pungent fragrance. Boo jumped down from the truck and took five steps before unleashing a mighty torrent.

I had previously visited Union Pass on my first annual camping trip with Tim. After several days of fishing, farting, and accumulating empty beer cans, we were visited by a family of aliens. Emerging from their interstellar starship (which was disguised as a minivan), they stunned us with their immaculate apparel and well-groomed appearance. With true diplomacy, Tim welcomed them with a universal greeting and emboldened their desire for data. They avoided this opportunity to share their intentions, invaded our camp, and showed no fear of two men spackled with layers of camping grime. While examining our earthly customs, the intergalactic travelers displayed a strange fascination with our dead fish. Either they had taken the wrong route to Yellowstone or were demonstrating a severe inability to mimic earthling behavior within a rustic Wyoming landscape.

Perhaps their visitation was related to the unique geographic contours of this location. Not far from Union Pass, the Continental Divide separates the headwaters of the Mississippi, Colorado, and Columbia rivers—a triple divide. A puff of wind can decide the ultimate destination for a single snowflake or drop of rain. For travelers from distant solar systems, this geographic triad is significant and may be a special nexus between this world and others.

Boo and I finished our dinners while a cool grey dusk spread its shadow over our surroundings. Then we took a short walk through the sagebrush. As far as I knew, she had never experienced the raw vitality of the mountains. She was inquisitive, yet cautious and stayed by my side. At the same time, she expressed a deep connection as she stood tall and stared into the distance. Darkness crept in, the night sky shimmered with bright starlight, and the whiteness beside me refused to fade.

Day two of our vacation began with a tour through Yellowstone while patiently cruising within a convoy of RV traffic. With her window rolled down and glimpses of scenery, Boo found enough distractions to maintain an air of satisfaction. For several hours, caravans of gawkers upstaged this majestic queen of the national parks. Eventually West Yellowstone fell behind us and our restless serenity returned along the thinly populated roads of southwest Montana.

At the junction of I-15 and Highway 43, we entered the Big Hole Canyon. This was one of my old playgrounds and I became nostalgic for past fishing and hunting adventures. Expeditions around Fleecer Mountain and the Big Hole River had occupied a large portion of my college life at Montana Tech. These almost took precedence over fluid mechanics and differential equations. I was tempted to visit my old haunts along the abandoned railroad on the far side of the river, but the winding two-lane highway offered the promise of rest and cold beer.

Later that afternoon, we rolled into our rendezvous site on the edge of a mountain meadow. Tim and Darrin were still elsewhere and Boo was already scouting around, so it was time to explore.

On the previous evening, Boo had proven her reliability within an unconfined wilderness. I dampened my caution and allowed her to roam without the restraint of a leash.

A small brook, defined by a line of willows, cut through the meadow and suggested a convenient fishing opportunity. I followed a direct path toward a gap in the willows while Boo meandered across the rocky soil sprinkled with wispy grass and timid wildflowers. The cool, clear water revitalized her spirit, but fish-wise, it wasn't promising. Then we continued to the other side of the meadow.

Upon reaching the shade of the bordering forest, we took a break beneath a tall fir tree. Suddenly, Boo got up and started barking and racing along the edge of the meadow. I kept calling her back to me and she faithfully returned before resuming her frantic behavior. I was pulling a leash from my pocket when I noticed what she was chasing. She was chasing butterflies. And the butterflies were winning.

When the Idaho boys arrived, two more dogs, Abby and Cliff, joined our gathering. Both had been raised on Tim's small farm. Abby was a middle-aged Chocolate Lab and Cliff was her overgrown puppy. He was taller than his mom and his lanky blond frame suggested a possible affair with a tall Golden Retriever. A stranger would never guess the two dogs were related.

Not long after their arrival, a new camp tradition was born: no dogs, except Boo, were allowed near my truck or my gear. My girl established this legal precedence and never offered clemency over the following years. If I couldn't see her around the camp, she was probably in the back of our truck, or under the tailgate, and enforcing her version of the castle doctrine.

Abby had no reason to interfere with Boo's business. Cliff was less compliant with her demands. Perhaps he thought it was a game. This became an odd species of love between the two dogs, but it seemed to work.

Even though the fishing never panned out, it was a good reunion with the boys and other dogs. After spending two days in the foothills of the eastern Bitterroot Mountains, Boo had become a solid camping companion and dedicated administrator of legal matters.

For our final night, we stayed in the Forest Service's Oreana Lookout, high on the Idaho side of the Bitterroot Mountains. There was no furniture in the lookout, so the boys and I staked out vacant spots on the floor among our dogs. On the following day, we woke up and filled our bellies with coffee and leftovers. The Snake River high country, bathed in hazy morning light, blended into the sky as Boo followed me to a narrow and weathered shack where I told her to wait outside. Then we loaded the truck and continued our fidgety trip to Boise.

PART TWO

I attended two weddings with Boo at my side. Although her name was missing on both invitations, she came along anyway. I had nowhere to leave her and didn't have a date.

Both weddings were in western Idaho and within the general area around Boise. I've driven between Denver and Boise too many times. Flying there is also an option, but this limits my zeal for excessive cargo and furry companionship.

The fastest route from Denver to western Idaho is to take Highway 287 up to I-80 in Wyoming, hop over to I-84 in Utah, then pursue a retreating horizon across the Snake River Plain in southern Idaho. This takes about fourteen hours and is one of the most painfully boring drives in the western US. When designing the Interstate Highway System, the engineers and surveyors selected routes where scenery was limited to travel brochures and rest area posters.

As we drove down from the lookout, Boo and I were well north of the direct route to Boise. We traveled south to Stanley then southwest around the imposing granite of the Sawtooth Mountains. Although hot springs abound in this area, we continued to neglect the need for cleanliness and kept moving down the road.

This was the final stretch of our meandering journey to southwest Idaho, where we would attend a wedding two days later. The groom was my old roommate, Triton. Back when I was a Boise resident, Triton and I shared a small two-bedroom house on West Idaho Street. His Rottweiler, Emma, had been a good buddy of mine and her huge grin displayed every tooth in her mouth. It looked like she was snarling, but it was just a big toothy grin.

When we arrived in Boise, Boo and I stayed with my friend Skully for the night. Our avoidance of bathing may have been offensive, so we spent the night in Skully's backyard. The next morning, as our bodies resumed ripening, we drove north to Cascade Lake and spent another smelly evening in the back of my truck. While I could have taken a shower back at Skully's place, I only had one set of clean clothes that were buried deep inside my supplies and reserved for the wedding.

The next day, we prepared for the wedding.

With the windows fully opened to reduce our exposure to ourselves, we made the short drive to the shores of Cascade Lake where we found an unoccupied beach. Our goal was to mildly contaminate the local water supply. I tossed a couple of sticks into the lake and this completed Boo's bath. Then it was my turn. Although Cascade Lake is fed by cold mountain streams, warmer water had accumulated in the shallows during the summer. Warmer, but not warm. The water stung my flesh as I dipped below its surface and swam briskly until the chill became tolerable. When I slowed down and coasted through the still water, Boo caught up and chugged along beside me. She was a good swimmer but was perplexed by my ability to swim. From the perspective of the water's surface, our heads bobbed along as if we shared a common aquatic ancestor. She never left my side and I truly believe she was trying to save me from drowning.

We swam back to the shore, toweled off, and dug out the clean clothes I had been saving for the wedding. It was a warm sunny day, so a short nap with a damp dog was necessary before changing my clothes.

The ceremony would take place at Payette Lake, a few miles to the north. Following a maze of state park roads and a few wrong turns, we found our assigned campsite. For Boo's attire, I tied a colorful Arapahoe Basin bandana around her neck. She looked rad and beautiful. Then I checked my face in the rearview mirror and removed a few crazy hairs. We were a perfect mismatched couple.

Triton's wedding was held along the twilight shores of Payette Lake. The setting was perfect for this occasion. As the solemn ceremony commenced, Boo launched into Boo-mode. I should have expected this. She was a shepherd dog and had been bred to guard and herd sheep. Apparently, we all looked like sheep and it was her duty to defend the gathering from any uninvited critters.

There must have been some coyotes or raccoons nearby because she was quite boisterous. Folks wondered in hushed tones, "Whose dog is that?" I pretended to be unaware of this concern. To avoid suspicion, I moved away from the crowd and hoped Boo would discretely follow me.

Perhaps it was unconventional to have a dog as a date for a wedding. But after extending the invitation to include my excitable companion, I was unable to change my fate. If, by chance, I had brought a woman instead of a dog, it might have been a more polite affair with fewer distractions and better suited for a fictional romance story.

Following the reception, Boo and I returned to our campsite and crawled into the bed of my truck. It would be a long, long trip back to Denver filled with the same anxious habits that were described previously.

SECOND WEDDING

It started when the Green River (then known as the Noname River) grew tired of flowing eastward and sought a southern path through the Uinta Mountains (then known as the Noname Mountains). While devouring multihued layers of prehistory, it realigned the Continental Divide and created the Flaming Gorge. Fifty years before Darrin's houseboat bachelor party, a towering concrete dam impounded the river near the Wyoming-Utah border and the Flaming Gorge Reservoir filled the upstream canyons and valleys.

After a quick stop in Rock Springs, Boo and I finally arrived at the Lucerne Valley Marina parking lot. Below us, large floating boxes were docked like side-by-side cargo containers. A pair of stout pontoons and a five-horsepower engine made each "house" seaworthy. Over the next few days, our friend Camille piloted the houseboat while the rest of us drank beer. For a bit of variety, we also played cards, fished, swam in the lake, and loitered around the upper and lower decks.

Boo and Cliff were the only dogs on the boat. This was a misfortune for our pups as they patiently waited to go ashore where they could address their needs. There was little else for them to do. I'm sure Boo's opinion of this "party" was well south of enjoyable, except for some dinner treats that included fresh trout and Ray's crawdad curry.

Darrin and Michelle's wedding would take place in Boise and was scheduled a few days after the bachelor party. With some time to spare, Boo and I took a detour to Notellum Lake in Idaho's Sawtooth Wilderness.

I lived in Idaho for nearly eight years and had done my

best to plunder its abundance of lightly traveled country. If I had an opportunity to escape Boise, I would fish the Boise River, ski in the backcountry, disappear into Owyhee County, or hike in the Sawtooth Wilderness. During this time, I schlepped over many trails in the Sawtooths. My primary incentive was the pursuit of elusive cutthroat trout while capturing memories with Kodachrome or Velvia film.

Six hours after departing Flaming Gorge, we found a place to camp near the Notellum Lake trailhead. The valley forest pulled Boo away from our camp and I was not far behind. Before long, I came upon a small creek filled with tiny kokanee salmon and one Australian shepherd. Like sockeye salmon, their cousins along the Pacific coast, the kokanees were bright red and green and had jaws that resembled fishy grimaces. Unlike sockeye salmon, the kokanee salmon were only five inches long. To associate them with any kind of salmon was ridiculous. They looked more like aquarium fish. And despite my efforts to catch a few appetizers, they showed zero interest in my angling skills. But it was a nice camp and, for the first time since leaving Aurora, we enjoyed a full night of rest.

Most hikes in the Sawtooths start with a long, leisurely gradient followed by a steep ass-kicking climb at the end. The trail to Notellum Lake was no different. It was a pleasant stroll for the first three miles and we barely broke a sweat. Then things changed.

If we had reached this spot twenty thousand years ago, there would have been a thousand feet of ice over our heads, maybe more. Above this glacier, a smaller tributary of ice flowed in from an upper valley. Near the intersection of these two glaciers, the smaller one paused and excavated Notellum Lake. Then they melted and disappeared down the Salmon

River. Instead of boring upward through tons of ice, our route led through a mile of fractured and sculpted granite.

There was one section of this ascent where the trail cut straight uphill through a thicket of alder bushes. The only way to conquer this steep corridor of vegetation was to grapple with the alders and use their bases like ladder rungs.

While assaulting the alder gauntlet, it started to rain. Heavily. I gripped the low-lying branches with one hand and pushed Boo's butt up the trail with the other. Then I balanced myself one foot higher and repeated the process. Even though this obstacle was less than thirty feet long, the slick rock and mud doubled the distance. After defeating the alder slip-n-slide, we were back on a more agreeable trail where Boo flushed a blue grouse and almost chased it off a cliff. And it continued to rain.

As we approached the lake, which sat in a rocky hanging valley near the timberline, the gradient leveled off. This new setting was completed when the rain froze and became a late-summer blizzard.

Retreat was not an option. I was here for one thing: to fish. Several years earlier, when Darrin and I had discovered Notellum Lake, we loaded our stringers with cutthroat trout. This excessive bounty forced us to pack more than five pounds of trout back down the trail.

I was ready for round two.

This time, I was horribly cold and wet. Slanting sheets of snow nearly obscured the lake. It took at least ten minutes to assemble my rod and tie on a fly. As soon as I finished this miserable task, I began slapping the slushy water with my fishing line. Fat snowflakes obscured the trajectory of each cast.

It was the dumbest thing Boo had ever seen.

I continued my insane behavior for several minutes before reason finally seeped into my frozen skull. Admitting defeat, it took another indefinite amount of time to stow my fishing gear inside my pack.

Our descent down the slippery slopes was worse than the climb. As the gradient became more level, we came to a log bridge that led over to the main trail. The rain was still coming down and the log glistened with the promise of an unintended bath in the creek. We chose to avoid catastrophe and waded across. To say we were saturated would be a feeble metaphor. It was pointless to avoid any of the puddles that now populated the trail.

I had a dry change of clothes back at the truck, but Boo didn't. Toweling and shaking were her only solutions. Then we dragged our shivering bodies into the truck and cranked the heat up to eleven. Four hours later, we rolled into Bernie and Madriene's place in Emmett. With less than two days to recover, I felt chills and fever brewing inside me.

By the day of the wedding, I was slowly regaining my health. To be honest, Boo and I didn't go to the wedding. Neither of us had brought formal attire. We only attended the reception where I enjoyed hot Boise sunshine and avoided beer like a seasoned teetotaler.

Boo was the only dog at the reception. This time, she behaved like an angel, stayed close to me, and didn't chase or scream at anything.

Darrin's bride was beautiful in her white wedding dress with a long flowing train. Near the end of the reception, I noticed several muddy paw prints decorating Michelle's train. Even though I appreciated the artfulness of the design, I chose to keep this admiration to myself.

NOSY NEIGHBOR

My townhome is also called a unit. When six of these are attached to each other, the resulting community is called a cluster. And our neighborhood is a conglomeration of many clusters.

Within each cluster, the garages face the center, like a three-sided square, with two garages on each side. A square slab of asphalt pavement is our shared driveway.

The purpose of this arrangement is to facilitate near-misses when we pull our cars out of our garages. This also hones our fifteen-point turning skills as we maneuver onto the main road.

I refer to the other residents within my cluster as my neighbors. And the neighborly configuration of our garages inspires us to introduce ourselves and complain about the HOA and other neighbors.

Over the years, many of these folks have moved to greener clusters and have been replaced by others who falsely assume my collection of power tools and lumber certifies my skills as a handyman. I've been the unofficial welcoming committee for too many years. It was a good place to raise Boo, and my roots are now deep.

It was Boo who introduced me to most of my neighbors.

The front of my garage, where the garage floor meets the asphalt, was Boo's lookout. She was discouraged from going beyond this boundary and would obey this rule until the priority of greeting a person or dog overruled her obedience. And there were times when pure curiosity also hindered her compliance.

Whenever I arrived home with Boo, I'd let her out of the

truck before lowering the garage door. Her next move was always toward the lookout where she could inspect the other garage doors to see if any were open. In her mind, an open garage was an invitation to visit and say hi to whomever she could find. If nobody was around, she would take the liberty of exploring their vacant garage. Most of my neighbors have been respectful folks and had learned to watch for Boo as she roamed between our units.

Every morning, as the rising garage door exposed the driveway, she performed the same routine. But the odds of discovering a morning invitation were quite low.

My garage also serves as a space for woodworking and storing things I rarely use. In other words, I must move my truck to another location before I can get any work done. To assure Boo she wasn't being abandoned, I'd say, "Just moving the truck. Ain't going anywhere." And she would understand.

With my truck stashed elsewhere, Boo might join me or remain inside the house. Her sleeping pad would be placed at the lookout if she decided to keep me company. Before settling in at the lookout, she would grab a walnut from a bucket along the wall, take it to the sleeping pad, crush the shell with her teeth, and snack on the exposed kernel. This was better than bringing walnuts into the house where the shards would torture my bare feet.

Tranquility was not common while I worked in the garage. My woodworking involves power tools and a bit of violence. "Beautiful" or "pretty" hardly describe my creations. There were times when poor planning interrupted my activity. Usually, my measurements had gone astray and I'd stare at my workbench while rubbing my face. These interludes allowed Boo to grab another walnut before returning to her neighborly observations.

A few of my neighbors also had dogs. One of these was Dave, who loved Boo and had no shortage of endearments. At the same time, his dogs fiercely resented my girl. They were never allowed much freedom and this may have corrupted their manners. Even though Dave was a curious character, he treated Boo with respect, so I guess he was OK.

Another neighbor, Debbie, owned a Chihuahua named Tess. Tess was very timid and, for her size, slightly plump. It was obvious this tiny girl wasn't a puppy, but Boo wasn't sure how to apply her rules of behavior. When they greeted each other, Tess would roll over onto her back and expose her tubby pink belly. Then Boo would lower her nose to fulfill her curiosity. That was the extent of their relationship.

Boo also introduced me to Bill and his wife, who lived in another cluster. On the night of our introduction, Bill was having a party to celebrate something and had left his back gate open. As we passed by during our evening walk, Boo slipped into his yard and found nothing but love and adoration from the partygoers. We were introduced to Bill's dog, Buddy, whom we already knew. Buddy frequently wandered around the neighborhood without supervision. Now we knew where this feisty mutt lived.

One afternoon, a year or so later, Boo confronted a bold coyote who had attacked Buddy. A few months after that, Buddy simply disappeared and never returned. Bill said he just walked away. The neighborhood had become too small for his wanderlust.

Straight across from our garage was a unit that had been a rental for a variety of tenants before it became a residence for a variety of owners. During its rental days, two guys who might have been auditioning for a soap opera added amusing drama to our cluster. I've forgotten their names, so I'll call them Butch and Blondie. They didn't have any pets and Boo tried to fill this void.

As neighbors we got along quite well. One time Butch saved me a trip to my mechanic when he replaced my sparkplugs. If they were having a fight, Blondie would invite himself into our house, pet Boo, and tell us the whole story. Like the time when he laid down in front of Butch's car to prevent him from leaving.

John and Athena lived next to this unit and had cats but no dogs. I don't remember when Boo and these folks became acquainted. It must have been when they left their garage door open for the first time.

Boo and Athena got along quite well. When their eyes met from across the driveway, they would dash toward each other and fall into a sloppy cuddle-fest. To pass the time, I would chat with John until their snuggling was completed—which could be a while.

Within their garage was a door which led into their house and never closed completely. Out of necessity, Boo modified her open-door policy to include those that could be pushed open. If their garage was open, she now had the authority to squeeze through the house door, look around for her girlfriend, and eat cat food.

John and Athena lived there for only a few years. One month after their departure, OT and Walter became my new neighbors. Boo continued to visit their house and did not understand the absence of her old friend. Although OT and Walter are great neighbors, they're not really dog people. It took a little patience and perseverance, but after a while, they accepted Boo as their new nosy neighbor.

NIGHT WALKS

My neighborhood is surrounded by acres of open space. This expanse of neatly mowed turf is also used for golfing. During the weekends, the golf course is teeming with hackers and can be a risky place for walking a dog. Snappy duck-hooks and stealthy shanks were real threats. To avoid any dimpled missiles that were launched in our direction, we used landscaping as cover and hugged the boundary along the townhouses.

Except in the middle of summer, when golfers pushed the limits of daylight well past our bedtime, the evening hours were more amenable to dogs and their human pets. Rabbits, owls, herons, nighthawks, bats, coyotes, and other critters also celebrated the exodus of roaming golf carts and snack wagon girls.

On our evening walks, we often ran into folks whom we recognized. These were the familiar faces. While all the dogs had names, the humans were denied this courtesy. Perhaps we had a common desire to remain anonymous.

Our usual greeting was "Hey, how ya doin'?" Then we would share long conversations about pets, families, politics, sports, philosophy, and the weather while maintaining indefinite identities. But there were awkward moments when I forgot a dog's name or gender.

Most folks prefer to shout their dog's name rather than their own and this was useful for learning a pup's name. Even the most shy and reserved people will bark like football coaches to rein in their unresponsive pets.

Anyway, during our nightly excursions around the golf course, it was nice to share some time with these folks whom

I never knew. Boo had no interest in these people or their dogs; socializing only interfered with her business. Her career path demanded more critical tasks, such as hunting bunnies or harassing slinky invaders.

On most of these evenings, we had the golf course to ourselves, especially when darkness claimed everything except porch lights and residential windows. While it was hard to conceal Boo's whiteness, we still enjoyed the comfort of being nearly invisible. If we saw someone illuminating their path with a flashlight or exposing their face with a glowing smart device, we would admire their bravery.

There were times when we passed by folks who appeared to be suffering from personal troubles and carefully slipped past their entourage of demons. On these nights, caution was another faithful companion. Once, on a very dark night, we nearly stumbled over a guy who was sitting against a tree. "Not smart to be walking around here in the dark," he said in a husky whisper. We just kept walking. Fast. Getting my front door between me and the outside world never felt better.

Despite the rare freaky encounters, these nightly walks were medicine for my soul. Workdays were a monoculture of surviving the grind inside an environmentally controlled cubical. After returning home, I would snarf a quick dinner, give Boo a treat, then forsake our modern comforts as we embarked upon brief adventures through a network of fairways and townhomes perched above a sea of streetlights splashing against the mountains. Even though heavy snow and blizzards could obscure the glittering metropolis, the glow was always present.

Boo would trail somewhere behind me or cover our

perimeter. Potential threats, like coyotes, or curiosities, like dancing poodles, drew her to the front. Offended gaggles of geese were emphatically evicted. And bunnies, afraid to risk fleeing toward cover, flattened themselves into the grass or snow as we passed. They were good at this. I would point at the vague fuzzy objects and whisper, "Bunny!"

A full moon on a clear night illuminated the golf course and created dark shadows. A cloudy night with snow on the ground reflected the city lights and bathed the nighttime in sepia. A clear night sky without moonlight or snow cover was deep black with stars shining brightly.

We shared very few evenings without a trip to the back-nine. I became familiar with the undulating patterns of the seasons and always knew the phase of the moon—even when it was hidden behind clouds or below the horizon. Waning and waxing were added to my vocabulary.

Living at an elevation above the metropolitan area was like having a balcony seat for distant thunderstorms. These sounded like bulldozers pushing boulders through an empty warehouse. Giant clouds, whose bellies were filled with fire, flashed on and off as they grumbled along. While I marveled at nature's misbehavior, this violence was racking up body shop and home repair bills for others who were sitting at center stage.

When the nighttime was calm and clear, I would gaze upward and wish I knew more about astronomy. I could always pick out the Big Dipper, the North Star, Orion, and, occasionally, his dog. A few times when the heavens were extremely clear, the Milky Way, our home galaxy, appeared as a faint smear of luminescence. And this was the extent of my celestial knowledge.

I had a sense of reverence for these dim crucibles of

stardust whose photons may have traveled for thousands of years before settling upon my retinas. Somewhere within this seemingly boundless universe, the tiny seeds of Creation had been forged and nurtured. I often wondered how a series of mystifying things, in the hands of God, could evolve into a guy walking his dog around a golf course.

COW VISION

White dogs are hard to see in the snow, especially at night. Boo's black eye patch and black ear betrayed her presence like two small blackbirds flying over the snow. If the moon was out, I'd look for her shadow. On dark nights without snow cover, she was a glowing white angel who glided beneath the heavens. These were the same dark nights that concealed the coyotes as they drifted nearby.

Then I discovered the art of cow vision. This might be a normal subconscious response that's activated when we stumble around in the dark. Developing this natural habit as a valuable talent was my generous gift to science.

Cow vision is simply staring ahead without focusing both eyes on a single point. It's like observing a full field of view without paying attention to any details. This enhances peripheral vision for detecting subtle changes of light and movement. Cows, with their expansive perception, are masters of this art. Therefore I named it in their honor.

All the same, my heightened awareness was usually old news. Boo's instincts humbled my emerging superpower. No coyote ever caught her off-guard.

Boo smelled the coyotes before either she or I saw them. They preferred dark, snowless nights for prowling through the neighborhood. With their natural invisibility, the coyotes were little more than ghosts. It was difficult to see them until they were only a few steps away.

If Boo began screaming into the darkness and her hackles were raised to high alert, I knew the coyotes were there... somewhere. Like a martial artist seeking strength from his inner core, I would summon my cow vision to locate the faint shadows. Although it worked quite well, my clumsy feet still compromised my superhero status.

Most of our encounters involved solitary coyotes. Pairs of coyotes might also introduce themselves. Sometimes there were more than two. The dark nights often prevented an accurate count.

Lone coyotes were simple work for Boo. Her absolute resentment of these critters often persuaded them to consider safer pursuits.

Not long after allowing Boo to range freely during our evening walks, a lone aggressive coyote materialized from the gloom and approached her. This wild creature had no respect for my girl's demands. Boo persisted in driving him off until both disappeared. By coincidence or intent, the coyote was leading her toward my house and the adjoining roads. Now the danger of feckless drivers had raised the stakes. My night walk had turned into a night run.

When I arrived back home, Boo was sitting by the front door with her antagonist pacing back and forth a few feet away. I asked the coyote to leave and without arguing, she turned away from us and slipped into the darkness.

Most coyotes look alike, and I can't tell one from the other. But there were a few who became familiar, so I gave them names.

Bonnie and Clyde were a dedicated team. Despite their poor manners when we shared a dark evening together, I admired their devotion and devious coordination.

Bonnie had a lame front leg and walked with a stilted gait. She may have enhanced this disability when playing her role as dog bait. Compared to Clyde and Boo, she was a small coyote.

I never saw Clyde until Boo went after Bonnie. Then he would reveal his plan as he closed in on my girl. If I saw Bonnie, I knew Clyde was nearby. The game was on. My cow vision would be activated at full intensity and Boo would take charge and spoil their deception.

How did I know Clyde was a boy and Bonnie was a girl? I didn't. But these names captured the dramatic nature of their characters. In fact, this was an odd assumption since female coyotes can be more aggressive toward dogs. Their maternal passion is centered on the security of their pups. When we examine the motives of the male coyote, we find a primal desire for girl coyotes—or girl dogs.

Which leads us to Freddy. To describe this lovelorn coyote, the word "desperate" might be appropriate. Boo was more literal: "What part of 'NO!' do you not understand?"

"Awkward" was another term that described Freddy as he crawled toward Boo one evening. She had no concern for his romantic suffering and offered a barrage of crippling responses. When she turned away to ignore him, he refused to accept her opinion and crawled closer. Then Boo whipped back around and invented a few more savage suggestions. Freddy was obviously a young coyote who was struggling with youthful desire.

We encountered Freddy two or three times, and he was always shackled with futile passion. His dreams were never fulfilled. Even though Boo was the most beautiful girl in the neighborhood, a tough little girl coyote would have been a better mate for him.

And Freddy wasn't the only coyote to fall for Boo's charmless charms. Over time, other coy-boys failed to quench their awkward rapture for my girl.

SACHI

I have never seen another Shiba who matched Koko in attitude and appearance. Her fluid conformation and atavistic nature resembled those of a wild dog. For social interactions, she defined her own morality and civic code.

Koko's fur was mostly a dark ginger color. Along her back and tail, wisps of black were blended with rusty-brown fur. It was a perfect symmetry of shade and color. Although the fur on her muzzle faded to white over the years, she had no other fur that was lighter than dark rust. This was unusual for a Shiba. Beneath this priceless coat, her skin was all black and her black tongue added emphasis to her ivory canines.

The Monkey Girl's tongue was used for eating, drinking, and grooming—not kissing. She didn't share Boo's fondness for face washing. If Koko suspected Boo was competing for my attention, she would resort to "almost kisses," where she barely touched my face with the tip of her black tongue.

Koko was also fiercely territorial. There were times when a passing stranger would admire the cute little doggy sitting inside my car. As each gleeful offender approached the danger zone, they were welcomed with snarling fury. Not one of these folks could control their sudden urge to retreat. They may have been unable to control other bodily functions as well.

I truly loved my Monkey Girl. She gave us many years of protection, excitement, terror, and love. My mom loved her deeply and her ferocious loyalty somehow found a soft spot inside my dad's heart. We knew she could never be replaced.

One month after Koko said her final goodbye, Boo and I visited my parents. Finding their house vacant, we continued into the backyard where they were playing with a chunky older Shiba who faintly resembled Koko. It was spooky.

Once again, Mom had returned to Dumb Friends and rescued a dog no one else wanted: a chubby eight-year-old brown Shiba who had been retired from a puppy farm.

Despite her lifetime of confinement, the runner instinct was strong in this dog. On the day after her adoption, the old girl disappeared. Somehow the plump elderly Shiba had escaped from their house.

"What? You're sure?"

"Yes, we're sure. We've looked everywhere."

I couldn't blame the dog. My suspicion leaned toward carelessness.

None of our girls ever ran away from us. They knew they had good homes. But there were days when the appeal of the great beyond was too compelling. Instead of running away, they chose to explore the unknown. As happy as they may have been with their adventure, we were impelled to find them. Entire neighborhoods were searched, strangers were interrogated, and shouting the dog's name became part of the ambiance. If my phone rang, I hoped for good news.

Mom's new Shiba didn't have a name and our voices were unfamiliar. Slowly driving up and down neighborhood streets was our only solution. With her advanced age and heft, she couldn't have gone far. The thought of losing another dog so soon after saying goodbye to Koko was crushing.

When this stressful day dragged into evening, Mom received a call from a woman with a Russian accent. She wondered if Mom was looking for a small brown dog. The chunky Shiba had trotted half a mile to Rosamond Park where she elicited concern from this saintly neighbor. This must have been the longest distance she had traveled on her own. Thankfully the rambling fugitive was wearing a Dumb Friends identification tag. When the woman contacted Dumb Friends, they provided Mom's phone number.

As soon as the Shiba was returned to my parents' home, the first order of business—following the elimination of all escape routes—was to give her a name.

Whether it was her appreciation of being rescued from involuntary service or simply part of her true nature, she was the happiest dog we had ever known. During her brief time as a new member of our family, she had never shown any emotion except complete joy. Mom took one look at her cheat-sheet of Japanese names and chose "Sachi" which means "happy little vanishing dog."

Over time, it became obvious that blaming my folks for Sachi's first solo journey was wrong. Disappearing was her trademark. And she loved every second of it.

Prior to being rescued by my mom, Sachi had probably lived inside a two-dimensional puppy mill world. For her, stairways and hills were new obstacles. While she was old enough to be a grandmother, she had never learned basic motor skills such as climbing and descending. Soon enough, though, she was incorporating a third dimension into her escape plans.

Lakes and creeks were new and foreign things as well. She learned how to wade into shallow water along the banks, cool off, and enjoy a little refreshment. If we were traveling along any deep water, I was confident these would not be included in her reconnaissance missions.

Although Sachi was a "runner," she had never learned how to run. Accelerating beyond a trot was not necessary inside a kennel. Over time, she developed a bouncy running style and looked like a big, awkward puppy. This was more than sufficient for her explorations. She already knew how to vanish without breaking a sweat.

She became fascinated by large animals like horses and deer. Even though she attempted to wear down her quarry with a steady trot, it was a struggle to keep up with her. Waiting for me was not included in her plans. And Sachi's compact body could go straight through wickets of deadfall and undergrowth that I had to avoid.

Of course, anything could seize her curiosity. During our walks, I would assume she was ten or fifteen feet behind me—and she usually was. This dependable behavior was a sham, but I refused to accept this fact. Calling her name never worked. Either confinement had damaged her hearing, or she didn't understand the concept of responding to a human voice. And when she trotted out of the woods, thickets, cattails, or any other relevant hiding place, she glowed with a satisfied exuberance that matched my anxiety. I've never known another human or animal who tested my patience with such cruelty.

Her deception reached its peak during several trips to the mountains where evasive opportunities awaited around each bend. With miles of wild country in all directions, she could have disappeared forever. The best strategy was to stop hiking and wait for Sachi to return. Therefore Boo and I would run up and down the trail until her mischievous grin would reappear exactly where it had vanished.

These adventures were the ultimate achievement for a Shiba who had spent most of her life in doggy lock-up.

On one of these trips into the hills, Sachi joined Boo, me, and my sister, Sara, on a hike up to Silver Dollar Lake near Guanella Pass. By this time, Sachi was becoming a regular mountain dog. She reigned in her sense of adventure and stayed within our sight. Having my sister along as a second set of eyes also helped.

Near the end of our lunch break, Sachi was lumbering up the trail behind a guy who was wearing jeans and a T-shirt. His attire resembled my own and perhaps this doppelganger had confused her. Sachi's departure had been calm and natural. Haste was not her thing. All the same, her absence wasn't noticed until my sister saw a small brown ball of fur trotting far up the trail. The dog had wiggled through a wrinkle in space-time. As she ascended the mountain, the thin air slowed her down and I quickly closed the distance between us. Upon seeing me, Sachi was quite confused about whom she should be following. Then she smelled a whiff of fried chicken on my fingers and followed me back to where we were having lunch.

ANOTHER TRANSITION

Sachi possessed a healthy set of lungs and powerful vocal cords that were used for two very loud demands: "Let's go!" and, more frequently, "Let's eat!" These edicts were amplified with emphatic bouncing and stomping. Any attempt to resist was like trying to ignore a flat tire.

She gave us over four years of goofy spirit and lost-dog blues. Every morning, like an overzealous ringmaster, she would announce the arrival of Boo and me. She thought my sleeping parents might appreciate this news while my dad grumbled about all the racket. She truly owned the word "ridiculous."

I'm not a morning person. I hate morning people and have no patience for cheery, bubbly nimrods while I'm trying to scrape the cobwebs out of my skull. But I love morning dogs. Most dogs are morning dogs. They've been waiting since midnight for their humans to show signs of life. Sachi was the epitome of a morning dog. For her, every day was Christmas. Somehow her comic relief softened the edges as I prepared for another day of cubical confinement.

Throughout the Sachi years, Boo was young enough to leap into my truck. Sachi's jumping style was more of a strenuous hop and she needed some assistance. She rejected my attempts to lift her into the truck, so this wasn't a solution. If I was parked near a curb, she could climb onto the floor and then up to the seat. Then I found a small plastic step that she used whenever a curb wasn't available.

The best solution was a doggy ramp. Some dogs require ramp training and others refuse to touch these gadgets. But not Sachi. She would leap onto the ramp as soon as I had it in position. OK, it was more like a vigorous hop.

It's been over ten years since we said goodbye to her. The ramp still has faint muddy outlines of her paw marks. As Boo got older and couldn't jump into my truck, I tried to encourage her to use the ramp. But Boo never learned to trust it. Although this contraption was no different from anything she had faced in agility trials, she didn't see the need for it—assuming her personal assistant had the strength to pick her up.

Now it's time to introduce another character in Boo's life: Yoshi. Let me begin with a short sketch then I'll go back to Yoshi's beginnings. For me, this is important, because she represents my current life as a doggy dad (or uncle).

As we rolled up to the Cherry Creek dog park, a traffic barrier was blocking the entrance. There was no explanation for closing the dog park, only a big striped barricade. So Yosh and I drove to the west side of the lake, where an unofficial dirt path ran along the shore. Autumn had introduced a chill to the morning and the swarms of mosquitoes that claimed this airspace had diminished into a few desperate bloodsuckers.

It had been ten months since losing Boo, and several months since I had looked behind me—where she should have been. Boo would have noticed the scent and offered security for her Shiba child. Without Boo, Yosh was left to her own devices as the wicked odor seized her attention. She stared into the brushy field. Her eyes were alert and her tail was low. Something inside the brush may have been looking back at us. I didn't see anything. She balked at continuing our journey and pointed her ears toward the truck. She often talks with her ears.

Even though Boo had shown Yosh how gain respect from coyotes, bad memories have tested the limits of her bravery. All the same, she is not a coward and we continued moving down the path. Soon her apprehension faded and she began investigating things that attracted her inquisitive nose. On the way back, we saw at least a hundred pelicans in the shallow water where the path came close to the shore. When we stopped for a break, Yosh jumped onto a large flat rock and posed for my camera. She's a natural poser. Then we resumed our adventure and finished another uneventful morning walk.

My mom cannot live without a dog. Going all the way back to when I first babbled, "Goggy!" she has experienced only a few years without a dog. There was Missy the Scotty, Gigi the poodle, Sasha the Siberian husky and her daughter Tamara, Nikki the red Siberian husky and her daughters Hunee and Nahni. And I've already mentioned Koko and Sachi. Oh, and Tigger, who thought he was descended from wolves.

When Sachi left us, Mom was getting older, but still wanted another faithful furry housemate. She thought a small foo-foo dog might be a reasonable choice. Among the more suspicious branches of the doggy family tree is a variety known as the Bichon Frise. This four-legged fluff-fest was frequently mentioned during our extensive assessments of various mutts. But the dog would be my responsibility as well, and such an animal would not join our family until hell Frises over.

I argued for a dog that weighed at least thirty pounds. Although this lacked scientific justification, it seemed to be appropriate for a dog that might go face-to-face with its wild cousins. Even a large pack of little yippy dogs could resemble Sunday brunch.

After establishing this premise, I suggested an Aussie. My reasoning was based on a simple fact: Boo was the perfect dog. I also reached out to a few Shiba breeders, since Shibas excel in nine out of ten "perfect dog" categories (their score for effective listening ranges between zero and point-zero-one). There is one distinct advantage to having a Shiba: they prefer to take care of their business in secluded areas, thus allowing it to remain untouched.

Mom took control of the matter and, by pure habit, visited Dumb Friends and other local pet shelters. This time, she failed to find an unwanted gem among the adoptable pets.

Having shared several wonderful years with a puppy-farm bitch, acquiring a puppy-farm puppy might have been slightly amoral. As fate would have it, Mom found a place called The Pet Ranch and came home with a skinny two-month-old Shiba. She was tan and white with dark, cunning eyes.

The Pet Ranch was a store that sold puppies, other pets, and sundry merchandise. The puppy farm connection was only an assumption. Independent breeders can be stingy about potential owners. Peddling their pups through a pet store was unlikely. If this small, tawny girl had come from a puppy farm, I'll never know. There was no reason to keep any record of her past. Mom had no desire to breed her. Nor would there be any obedience or agility events in her future. The puppy was simply Mom's companion.

She was my mom's first puppy in over twenty years. With this in mind, I was somewhat concerned about Mom raising a fearless beastling. Although this puppy had the physical appearance of a Shiba, there must have been a rascal or two somewhere in her lineage. Her overabundance of spirit was proving to be a terrible thing to endure, so Mom promptly gave her an appropriate Japanese name: Yoshi. A rough translation of this name would be "Spawn of Godzilla."

Boo loved puppies. She could be indifferent or defensive around adult dogs, but young pups always captured the ageless youth of her spirit. And she understood the difference between small adult dogs and puppies. Mature pugs, chihuahuas, and other toy dogs were encouraged to submit to her law with no exceptions.

Thanks to Dumb Friends' neutering policy and Boo's troubled genetics, she would never have puppies of her own. But now she had the next best thing. At the age of nine years, Boo finally had a young Shiba to raise and nurture. And this instantly cured her puppy love.

MAD SCIENCE

Yoshi's puppy teeth were unusually large for a little dog, and she employed these fearsome daggers without mercy. Few animate or inanimate objects could escape the wrath of her slashing canines. Even though she inflicted us with a variety of flesh wounds and destroyed hundreds of dollars of property, we still gave her our love.

After a few months, she was allowed to join Boo and me on our walks. When this privilege was granted, Yoshi wore a puppy halter and was constantly on a leash.

Her initiation into our club included a diabolical plan. I was determined to create an amphibious Shiba. While this might be worthy of a Nobel Prize and similar accolades, it was also necessary. Boo was an expert swimmer and sometimes our walks required swimming skills to navigate across streams and creeks. Our previous Shibas, Koko and Sachi, had to be captured and carried over any water they couldn't wade. Yoshi would not receive this concession—unless I ran out of options.

Below Cherry Creek Lake, the creek winds back and forth in a string of pools, runs, and riffles. This was the ideal setting for my experiment. With Yoshi attached to a long leash, Boo and I would wade across moderately deep channels while leaving Yoshi on the far bank. At first, her natural Shiba fear of wavering surfaces overruled the importance of crossing the creek. When we came to sections where Yoshi could feel the bottom, minimal effort was required to coax her across. She started to enjoy the cool water on her belly. Then we moved onto deeper crossings where a combination of coaxing and forcefully pulling her into the creek inspired her to churn through the water as if she were trying to split the creek in half.

During these early swimming sessions, she never tried to bounce off the bottom with her hind legs. Instead, she swam perfectly and used her hind legs along with her fore legs to propel herself through the water.

When learning how to swim, some pups will bounce off the bottom in lieu of proper aquatic technique. As long as the water isn't too deep, their hind legs will be employed as underwater pogo sticks until they finally figure it out. Other dogs are natural swimmers, like Boo and Yoshi. And then there are those, like Koko and Sachi, who refuse to enter any water that threatens their equilibrium.

Yoshi's dog-paddling finesse was a credit to her Spitz heritage. Phase one of my aqua-puppy experiment was a proven success.

To crown my achievement, I began throwing her into ponds and deep pools along the creek. Yes, this might seem harsh, but she would flawlessly swim to the surface, execute a turn, and paddle back to the shore.

Although she still hates swimming, I continue to devise situations that test her natatorial development. She has yet to fail any of these. And there have been times when she has taken a swim without provocation or consideration.

The next lesson would address the importance of reliable behavior without a leash. This was our toughest lesson and beyond the scope of any experiment. It was about survival.

While swimming required a bit of coercion, Yoshi had natural runner instincts. When she was a puppy, she escaped into my parents' front yard where a rambling gang of children chased her into the neighborhood. A year later, Mom was walking through a south Denver neighborhood with a leash that was hooked onto an empty collar. Yoshi didn't wait to resolve this problem. Both times, we searched too many side streets with our guts tied in knots. Both times, I found her in a neighborhood park and playing with other dogs. And both times, she was excited to see me. This was a hint of progress.

On the second escape, our pint-sized truant ended up in Bible Park, where she had discovered another dog who was leashed to its owner. While playing with her new friend, she also frustrated the sworn duty of an animal control officer. His over-sized net consistently captured patches of grass that Yoshi had just vacated. The comedy of her playful evasion allowed my stress to unwind into welcomed amusement. Fearing this exertion might strain the officer, I shouted her name and she happily ran back to me. Yes, she listened to me. I wish I could recall another time when she has responded to my voice.

Then there was the day when she jumped out of my car and into a parking lot that sat next to a busy street. The potential dangers of this escape still haunt me. Had it not been for the well-intentioned folks who were trying to catch her, the situation might have been easier to control. They were driving her toward the street when I loudly warned them about their terrible strategy. As the mob dispersed and offered a safer path, the satisfied wild-child ended her drama and trotted back to me.

This was the initial phase of our education. Unlike human schooling, there was no coursework—just test after test after test. Most of these were accidental, others were more deliberate.

One morning when she was growing into the stature of a young dog, the rising sun perfectly captured the golden hue of her coat against a dry summer hayfield. She glowed with pride and confidence. I removed her leash and stepped back to capture the moment with my camera. The resulting image was magical. It encapsulated the next twenty minutes that Boo and I wasted while chasing her around the field.

As a young girl, Yoshi never enjoyed surrendering her freedom. The chase was more of a game than existential necessity. She would often taunt me by staying inches beyond my reach. Escaping was never part of her plan. At the same time, she gradually expanded her boundaries.

Her passion for adventure soon exceeded that of Boo, Koko, or even Sachi. A smidge of loyalty anchored a generous umbilical for her wanderings. She didn't need any rules until they became good ideas.

But I adopted many rules during Yoshi's (and the other girls') off-leash training. Here's a quick summary:

Always have a leash. (Walking a dog while using my belt as a leash has always resulted in severe trouser slippage).

Always have a bag of her favorite treats. (This will make you popular with all the other dogs as well).

Always keep towels and hand sanitizer in the truck (for them and you).

Always be willing to tackle a little dog like you're in the NFL.

To address the dangers of thin ice, always train over shallow water that's less than a foot deep. Hopefully this will discourage any temptation to walk across icy ponds and creeks.

Always keep a record of where deep water can be found

(for removing any nasty stuff that has been joyously rolled in).

Always be as silent as possible when looking for a lost dog, while occasionally calling their name. (If they know where you are, there's a good chance they'll keep doing whatever they're doing).

Always hope for the best and be prepared for the worst.

Never get mad. (The times when I've lost my temper are not good memories).

Obedience training is a grind and might seem silly but can be valuable as well.

I also recommend snake training. Boo and Yoshi's training included defanged rattlesnakes and shock collars. It's a painful lesson, but far better than being bitten by a real rattlesnake. To reinforce their fear of snakes, I'll use wild bull snakes whenever the opportunity arises. Bull snakes will mimic rattlesnakes and this doesn't require a shock collar.

And the list continues to grow.

ANIMAL CONTROL

PART ONE

To prevent dogs from becoming our masters, we must enforce and obey animal control rules and regulations. If we fail to strictly adhere to this task, our clothes will be replaced with collars and bandanas, our wallets will become rabies tags and nametags, and our email will be downloaded onto signposts and bushes.

To be honest, I'm ambivalent about letting dogs run loose. Regrettable things have happened, or have almost happened, when Boo and the other girls pushed the limits of their freedom. It's a perilous world and they will face unforeseen dangers.

In retrospect, life with Boo and her various packs was a carefree and rewarding journey, but there were a few bumps in the road. Whenever she was out of my sight, I was cautiously optimistic. Although her hearing impairment proved to be a minor disability, my nature required a touch of apprehension.

Roaming freely is different from the freedom offered inside a dog park. If someone is inclined to let Scruffy run free, they should use the dog park as a test area. These places have risks as well. There can be frozen ponds, flooding creeks, snakes, poisonous toads, other dogs, and other dangers. Nuisances such as cheat grass, foxtails, goat heads, burdocks, cacti, mud, and smelly things can be unpleasant. Beyond the dog park, these dangers and annoying things increase by an order of magnitude. The absence of secure barriers requires obedient and vigilant behavior. I've often ignored this important detail myself.

I'm a sucker for a dog's free spirit. Independence fuels their souls, tests their resolve, rewards their intelligence, and punishes their errors. It improves social skills and inspires them to perform disgusting activities that would be denied inside a controlled environment.

In my opinion, allowing dogs to run free reinforces their confidence and emotional stability. Dogs who are restrained with leashes can be limited in their reactions. If this is their only taste of freedom, they can become defensive, protective, and, possibly, insecure. But that's only my opinion.

PART TWO

Cherry Hills Village begins at the top of a south Denver ridge that separates Goldsmith Gulch from the South Platte River. With an envious view of the Rockies, this suburban village descends through opulent estates, elegant enclaves, open fields, and natural swales until it gradually levels off at the Cherry Hills Country Club.

This is a metropolitan hamlet of upper-class real estate. Some of the homes inside the Village can be mistaken for medieval castles or European villas. Others are more austere and include large pastures, barns, and stables for raising horses. But most are tastefully crafted homes that congregate within subdivided estates.

Over the years, this refined, yet rural community has been our prime target for nurturing primitive behavior. Our favorite targets inside the Village include the High Line Canal Trail and the nearby open space on the Kent Denver School property. My history of dog expeditions within the Village began in the eighties and nineties when my companions were my parents' "grandchildren," Nikki, Hunee, and Nahni.

There's a small parking lot across from the canal trail that provides access to the eastern side of the school. This has been the preferred launching point for our morning operations. Tall cottonwoods bordering the parking lot provide shade and help conceal the initial phase of our covert activities. True criminals are also drawn to this spot, so it's advisable to leave the pretty Lexus at home and take the old Taurus instead.

As I've noted, Nahni was still with us when I came back to Denver. Koko, Nahni, and I frequently violated the animal control laws of Cherry Hills Village. On these walks, Nahni was the naughty one and always—or at least mostly—on a leash. The old husky could loosen my shoulder joints whenever a shiny four-legged object came into our view. One time, she broke free and loped off toward a coyote. When the coyote swam across the canal, she paused and I grabbed her tail. Another time, she broke free and joined two equestrians as they rehearsed their dressage. When I say, "broke free," I honestly don't remember whether she was on a leash or not.

The Village's commitment to enforcing its puppy laws is serious. Their records of our doggy delinquency began with an impressive show of force.

On that infamous day, Nahni, Koko, and I were starting our walk along the canal trail when a Village patrol car pulled up behind us. Although this path had evolved into a biking and pedestrian trail, it was originally designed for canal maintenance. Utility trucks still traveled along the trail for tree-trimming and general maintenance. But a patrol car? I blamed it on bad timing.

Less than thirty seconds after the cruiser had rolled in on our blind side, another patrol car came around the bend and prevented our escape from the front. This classic shock-and-awe pincer strategy was more than a simple coincidence.

I felt like a true criminal—an unrepentant threat to society. For a moment, I entertained the idea of running off the path and fleeing into an open field. We were screwed, so why not make it worthwhile? I could see the headlines: "Fugitive Puppy-Law-Breaker Escapes!" But Nahni, who was becoming a senior citizen, could not run very fast and might have been left behind as evidence.

I accepted fate and was presented with a citation for violating the "dogs at large" ordinance. The penalty was fifty bucks per dog and our neglect of civil conformity was immortalized within the Village's case files.

Being slightly rebellious and stubborn, I continued to let the girls roam freely within the Village. At the same time, I was more cautious. Several years went by before additional offenses were added to our doggy outlaw record.

PART THREE

Officer John was an enigma. For us, he was the face of animal control within the Village. His stone-clad nature was as easy to read as a petroglyph. Most of the time, he was a fair but strict law-enforcer with a measure of reason and compassion. And he was generous with warnings and not shy about threats when pushed too far.

Our cat-and-mouse game rose to a new level when he busted out his mountain bike to investigate areas where the patrol cars couldn't go. His dedication to his job went beyond anything I'd call reasonable.

My total respect for law enforcement hasn't cured me of occasionally ignoring the law. To this day, Yoshi and I still return to the scene of our crimes because it's a convenient and incomparable spread of open space.

Our meddling in John's business began in the Koko and Boo years. These dalliances continued through the Boo and Sachi years and then the Boo and Yoshi years. It became a lengthy relationship; perhaps I should have sent him a few Christmas cards. Here are a few of our more memorable engagements.

In the pre-mountain-bike years, he simply staked out the parking area and surveyed the surroundings with his binoculars. After observing our suspicious activity, he would patiently wait for our return and provide some advice before issuing a warning or citation. I believe we got one citation from this method. And I always refer to myself in the plural while describing these situations; I can't take all the blame.

Over time, we got wise to his tactical preferences. One morning, when Boo, Koko, and I were completing our tour of the Kent School grounds, this knowledge proved its worth. As we approached an exposed field, I studied the premises and caught a glimpse of the animal control truck in the parking lot. When I reached for my leashes, which I almost always carried, my pockets were empty. Evasive action was necessary.

Using all available cover, including a swamp and the empty bed of the High Line Canal, we took a stealthy and circuitous route until we were within twenty feet of our truck. When we peeked over the edge of the canal's bank, John had abandoned his post. We would be free for another day.

Inclement weather rarely discouraged our plans. When the temperature dropped to near or below zero, we had to move quickly to stay warm. On one of these frigid mornings,

Sachi, Boo, and I were jogging along the canal trail to keep our blood flowing. The temperature was hovering between the positive and negative digits. Other than us, there were no signs of life. It was hideously cold.

The winding trail had many blind spots where trees and shrubs obscured its path. As we came around one of these bends, we spotted the animal control truck parked along the trail. Ignoring possible damage to our fragile privileges, we continued toward the idling truck. I mean, who were we offending? The Norse god of shriveled parts? Apparently John saw no offence either and had no reason to exit his warm and toasty cab. We waved as we jogged by and he didn't even roll his window down.

Yoshi was an adult by definition when we violated Kent School property during the school's graduation day. The Village's "at large" infractions were also enforced on the school grounds. In addition, there was a special rule that was only effective during graduation day: interlopers who were not associated with Kent School were guilty of trespass. In other words, grungy dog walkers were not allowed to intrude upon this prestigious occasion—like the day when Koko took a detour through the graduates' reception tent while looking for handouts.

This time, Boo and Yoshi were flaunting Village rules in two different directions. John was parked above us and below the Head of School's home. His indictment rang clearly from the patrol car's bullhorn: my dogs did not meet the definition of "under control." Then he mentioned something about trespassing, but I was too busy trying to address his first concern. Getting Boo on a leash was a simple task; she was a very good girl. Yoshi, on the other hand, had decided to act like a little brat. I dropped Boo's leash, chased after Yoshi, enticed her with treats, and tackled her. My frustrated efforts must have been horribly amusing and this prevented him from documenting any criminal activity.

Boo had become eligible for social security benefits when she committed her final offence. We were crossing the bridge at the parking area when the animal control truck pulled in right behind us. John bleeped his bullhorn and I felt like an idiot. After all these years, I had let my guard down at the most obvious location. Leaving Boo on the bridge, I crossed over to the trail and calmly told Yoshi to wait. She was older now and had learned to obey—when she wanted to obey. This time, she reverted to being an ornery little shit.

As soon as Yoshi was "under control", our misbehavior continued to escalate. Using his stern and offended voice, John shouted, "Your dog is crapping on the bridge!" Sure enough, when I turned toward him, Boo was flagrantly desecrating the bridge as he stood over her. Once again, he showed mercy and didn't press any charges. He also let me know I was beginning to piss him off. Just beginning? Like I said, he could show admirable restraint.

As one would expect, this wasn't the last of our engagements. These might include a few more warnings and maybe another citation—and a growing case file at city hall.

THE COUNTRY CLUB

Despite the legal risks associated with daily "at large" behavior, the girls and I have accumulated a good number of bonus miles within the Village. Rewards have included wild berries, apples, asparagus, mushrooms, and various species of vermin. Of course, the best reward is sharing the trail with the happiest furry renegades on the planet.

Within the school grounds, we often ran into folks—and their dogs—who had become our friends. We were not the kind of friends who socialized in trendy hangouts or shared emoji-flavored social media posts. We simply enjoyed breaking the law together. I even knew a few of their names.

Art and Leslie had a big girl malamute named Malika and a big boy malamute named Denali. For most of Boo's life, we had similar schedules and our paths frequently crossed. Malika was fluffy and beautiful and made funny noises when I scratched her back. Boo would ignore my silly infatuation with the big girl, trot away, and share some time with Art.

Art always packed doggy treats. Even though Yoshi is suspicious of most people—with good reason—she would shamelessly compete with Boo to snag a portion of his stash.

Eldridge and his Labrador retriever, Iris, were both friends and formidable foes. Asparagus grew throughout the school property and our preference for certain areas became tribal. We eventually settled on terms that gave me the south side of the Kent School. Regardless of my good intentions, there was a slight issue with this treaty: I had to cross his territory to get back to my truck and ignoring freshly sprouted asparagus was an arduous mental task. He only caught me once.

For the girls and me, the Kent School was a wild country club. To distinguish it from the elegant and nearby Cherry Hills Country Club, it simply became the "Club." Membership was extended to folks who willingly accepted the possible consequences. Uncontested citations covered our club fees.

Enjoying my own independence was also important. This was my excuse for letting the girls run loose and allowed me to gather certified organic produce while the girls did whatever they did. Most of the time, they would watch me with sub-curious boredom.

Whenever the climate offers acceptable proportions of warmth and humidity, a variety of mushrooms will sprout in the open fields and shady nooks. Those that are fit for the frying pan include meadow, fairy ring, slippery jack, oyster, and shaggy parasol mushrooms.

In good years, a half-pound of fairy ring mushrooms can be plucked from the fields during a morning walk. Unlike other mushrooms, which spoil quickly or become ravaged by pleasing beetles, fairy rings persist through the summer as if they possessed a secret gnomish elixir.

The shaggy parasols, which have a strict preference for perfect late-summer conditions, make the best mushroom burgers. The tangy flavor of the slippery jacks is enjoyed as soon as I free them from the earth. My prize find is always the oyster mushrooms. I keep their locations confidential and shed various layers of outerwear to adapt to their sloppy harvesting conditions.

Amanita mushrooms appear in late summer and are abundant after a heavy monsoon season. Although they can be photogenic, they may be extremely poisonous as well, so I leave them alone.

Over the years, Club privileges have also been granted to the local coyotes. If their presence becomes a public nuisance, their membership status might be revoked by the animal control folks. Cherry Hills Village should have given Boo and Koko some credit for maintaining peace and order among the coyote population. But we never received a certificate of achievement and the Village continued to discourage our "at large" privileges.

One of my favorite pictures has Boo and Koko staring across the upper pond on a winter morning. Both girls have a look that suggests business. Serious business, but also mysterious. On that day, I couldn't see what held their attention. Perhaps they were displaying their authority to whomever may have been watching them. They thought they owned the place and had no sympathy for the coyotes' aboriginal rights.

Like people, dogs desire a sense of importance and respect. The greatest gift for my girls was the right to assert their independence. Although the consequences could be tough, their spirits never suffered.

Boo and I had been together for only a few months when our first coyote encounter occurred along the canal trail. She and Koko were trotting ahead of me. Their leashes remained inside my pocket. As we approached a patch of willows along the path, two coyotes suddenly appeared. Koko and Boo saw them before I did.

The Monkey Girl ignored my shouts and pursued them into an overgrown meadow. Boo hesitated and was quickly restrained with a leash. When Koko discovered her lack of support, her impulse faltered. She stood on her hind legs like—well, like a monkey—to survey the area above the tall grass. There was nothing for her to see. With her foes concealed somewhere nearby, Koko abandoned her folly. As I dragged both girls back to my truck, Boo was beside herself and screaming at the empty field. I was unaware of her enmity for these cagey critters, but it soon became obvious.

A few years later, in this same area, Boo and I ran into a woman whose morning schedule had been disrupted by the intimidating presence of a coyote. The preoccupied creature was a stone's throw away from us and just off the canal trail. He appeared to be hunting voles or bunnies. All the same, I let my girl handle the situation. Boo didn't need my permission and was already issuing a severe warning to the startled animal. In response, the coyote trotted away from the trail before disappearing into a thicket. The woman appreciated Boo's fearless assistance and continued her walk. Once again, the Village failed to notice Boo's selfless dedication to civic service.

DAY SCHOOL

Unlike Boo, Sachi held no grudges against coyotes. She never bothered them and they never bothered her. One time, she trotted through a pack of four coyotes while grinning as if everyone had missed the punchline. I expected trouble, but all I saw were some very confused critters. It was almost like they had witnessed a supernatural being.

In fact, the Club's coyotes rarely displayed any emotion except indifference. This docile behavior added a measure of surprise whenever they attacked without provocation.

I had heard about coyotes ambushing dogs, but this was only a rumor until I saw it for myself. Similar to the tactics of our friends Bonnie and Clyde, one coyote posed as dog-bait before others emerged from the shadows and attacked from the rear.

The ambushes occurred without warning. Maybe that's a redundant statement, but a pleasant excursion could quickly disintegrate into a clash between the tamed and untamed. Defending these attacks was beyond my ability. I was a consultant, not an Olympic athlete.

There were times when this wily behavior backfired.

One of these started with Boo chasing a coyote along the edge of a field that was bordered by cottonwoods and dense shrubs. As they vanished through a break in the trees, a second coyote revealed himself and chased after Boo. About fifteen seconds later, the two felons came back into view with their tails held low. Their retreat was hastened by Boo's commitment to justice and her distaste for bad manners. Yes, they got an earful of good advice.

Several years later, Sachi and I were approaching a gap

where the trail cut through a brushy swamp. Boo was ahead of us and on the other side of the gap. She was hidden behind a shroud of vegetation and explaining the rule of law to an invisible nemesis. From the tone of her voice, I knew it was a coyote. A few seconds later, in the middle of the gap, another coyote raced out of the thicket with his nose pointed toward Boo's direction.

When Sachi and I appeared in the corner of his eye, he turned toward us and froze. While this guy was questioning his motives, another conspirator sprang from the brush with unhinged momentum, collided into his buddy's midsection, cartwheeled through the air, and landed on his back. It was like a Road Runner cartoon. Their badly executed assault was a total bust. It wasn't long before Boo, who was still on the clock, reunited her cowering student with his recovering comrades and demanded their immediate departure.

After a rigorous morning of chasing fauna and frisbees, it's always good to have a place to cool off.

The Club has two ponds, the upper and lower Blackmer Ponds. These were developed when this area was known as the Blackmer Farm. Both ponds were constructed to endure many generations. The upper pond is more of a small lake where dogs will ignore the "No Swimming" sign. The lower pond offers less access for swimming and is more congested with trees and shrubs.

The elevated banks on the upper pond can be used as launch pads for doggy diving. While the Shiba girls never saw the need for this sport, Boo loved to fly off the bank and loudly splash into the pond. As her assistant, I would toss a toy into the water and watch her sail through the air. She only mastered one dive, the belly flop, but got high scores every time.

When the ponds freeze over during the winter, they can become treacherous. To lessen the risk, I trained Boo by leading her over thin ice that concealed only a few inches of water. She learned quickly and even avoided frozen puddles. Yoshi had a slower learning curve. Initially, she used the frozen ponds as wide-open doggy highways for her winter adventures.

This was an issue with Yoshi for one or two winters. She weighed less than thirty pounds and might have been light enough to avoid any danger. Whenever I threw a stick onto thin ice that posed little risk, she would trot over the frozen surface and come back unscathed. If she did break through, the water would be too shallow and fail to curb her fearless impulses.

She finally found a perfect training site on the upper pond. Luckily the water was shallow enough to be safe and deep enough to be useful. As the ice fell away beneath her, she was struck by a healthy wave of panic before clawing her way up the bank.

Whenever we approach risky situations, I will use the command "careful." This wasn't taught through normal training. The command only became effective after Boo or Yoshi had associated "careful" with "don't do anything stupid." To add assurance, I'll often include the command "wait."

The word "careful" became part of Yoshi's vocabulary on a cold and snowy day on the eastern end of the Club. Up to this point, she had been hunting rabbits inside the overgrown swales with impunity. These were nasty uncharted habitats filled willows, chokecherries, Russian olives, and cattails. One of these thickets had concealed the coyotes who ripped into

Boo's backside a few years earlier.

On this winter day, Yoshi's path was uncertain. I shouted warnings toward her assumed location and hoped she was listening.

A lack of response fueled our impatience and concern. Then her screaming filled the small valley. She was a hundred yards away and near a known coyote den. A Shiba scream is a terrible thing to hear. It's shrill, loud, and penetrating. What I heard that day was worse.

Boo was unable to determine the direction of Yoshi's terrible screams, so I took the lead. This hindered our progress through the stubborn vegetation and slick ice. It was a nightmare of frustration. When we came upon Yoshi bravely confronting a menacing coyote, I felt a hesitant sense of relief.

Boo charged forward and added self-preservation to the coyote's agenda. Yoshi used Boo's intrusion to limp back to me. Blood covered her face and neck. It was now a contest of maternal passions. Boo held her ground just feet away from the snarling bitch. The aggression never became physical, but the standoff was furious. Although the coyote fiercely defended her den, she was wary of Boo's presence.

Yoshi and I started walking back to the truck as fast as possible while Boo held the coyote at bay. I yelled at Boo and she cautiously retreated. As soon as we were safely inside the truck, I made a quick call to our vet and another to my mom.

Yoshi and I were lucky. She had lacerations on her neck and shoulder. A puncture wound on her neck had barely missed a major artery. Surprisingly, she had no injuries to her face. The blood I had seen there must have come from the coyote.

As she was recovering, a dose of mange appeared

around her jaws. But this was treatable and relatively minor.

It was several years before Yoshi was willing to go back to this section of the Club. It had been a really tough lesson for both of us.

Experience may be the best and only teacher. The girls and I often followed trails where advice had never tread. If we got tangled up in a mess, we became educated. Some folks call this a teachable moment, but I doubt these stories will ever find their way into a textbook.

THE HUNTING CLUB

PART ONE

Most of the Kent School property is a working hay farm that winds around ponds, brushy drainages, athletic fields, and school buildings. This pastoral anomaly is tucked inside the ritziest neighborhood in Colorado where the preferred mom cars are Cadillac Escalades. Irrigation for this farm is limited, so the harvest depends on favorable weather. The inventory of hay can be impressive during wet years and dry years might produce only a few meager bales.

It's a one-man operation. Farmer Mel harvests the hay, maintains the irrigation system, and lives in a different era. His passion for tinkering with vintage farming equipment is obvious. There have been times when Mel's collection of vehicles and machinery has resembled a small Midwestern boneyard, but most of it still works. An old Hydro Swing 1014 must have finally exceeded his patience for fixing things and was abandoned where it had laid down its final row of hay.

The temperature had climbed to over ninety degrees during one of our weekend walks on the west side of the Club. Boo was getting older, our pace was slow, and breaks were frequent. We were about two hundred feet past Mel's boneyard when the heat finally stopped her from going any farther.

Mel was wrenching on his machinery when he saw me carrying Boo back down the path. He dropped what he was doing and came over to help. With Mel leading the way, I carried Boo to a water pump and splashed cold water onto her belly. This helped significantly and she began to recover.

"Where are you parked?" Mel could see we still needed his assistance.

"At the end of the horse trail."

"Wait here. I'll get my ATV."

Yoshi refused to ride on Mel's strange vehicle and even appeared fearful. She might have followed us, but I wasn't in a mood to experiment. While Boo and I rode on the back of the ATV, I used a long leash to troll Yoshi back to my truck.

Mel is the unofficial professor of farming and mechanics at Kent School. His teachers' lounge is a utility truck. Grading midterm reports and final exams are not part of his job. He teaches by example. This ephemeral education is not included within the school's curriculum, which may lean toward more gentrified careers. But he taught me something about generosity and I hope he doesn't mind going onto my list of angels.

Mel's boneyard is also where he stores the hay. His old, oily harvesting equipment and fermenting bales of hay are contiguous with the school's maintenance buildings, related machinery, piles of tree limbs from trimming projects, and an evolving junkyard of old school stuff. All the local rabbit wranglers refer to this expanse of chaos as "happy, happy bunnyland."

Once a dog has discovered bunnyland, she may never wish to leave. Unless she's chasing a hightailing bunny. Most dogs only dream about places like this or read about them in *Burks Afield.*

The girls have always been allowed to range freely around bunnyland. A favorite bunny sanctuary is beneath a large dumpster where my companions would doggedly circle the perimeter. Even though the security of this bunny bunker is undeniable, sometimes a cottontail would dash from the dumpster and safely toward the woodpile where the siege would begin anew.

Personally, I had no interest in the girls' success or failure. I'd give them ten minutes or so, then walk away from bunnyland and hope loyalty and frustration were sufficient reasons to follow me. If their devotion wasn't certain, I would discover the benefit of the "at large" rule and pull out the leashes.

PART TWO

Within this small and shallow valley, the uncut hay fields bordered by pines and cottonwoods may resemble what Denver looked like before country clubs, dinner parties, and municipal codes. Swampy tendrils of thick brush frame individual fields and provide cover for the local inhabitants. After the harvest, the mowed fields appear barren, but the Club is still filled with life.

A few wild predators and their prey call this place home. As I've noted, coyotes are quite common. While foxes and raccoons are also present, they are not as prevalent in the fields as they are in the surrounding neighborhoods. Over the years, there have been a few cougar sightings as well, and this is a sobering fact.

Bull snakes slither, hide, and hunt in the deep grass. Mornings might find them sunbathing in the middle of a trail. These are constrictors, like small pythons, and can grow to over six feet long. A bull snake may not be as threatening as its jungle relatives, but a crowbar could be handy if one is wrapped around an arm.

Rattlesnakes might be present as well. My mom and one

other lawbreaker are my only sources for this claim. There's a rumor that bull snakes kill rattlesnakes, so seeing a fat momma bull snake is a reassuring sight.

Little tarantulas are the most unlikely predatory inhabitants. They are about an inch long and perfectly ugly. One time I came upon a momma tarantula whose back was bristling with baby spiders. It looked like a big spider with squirmy warts. Again, perfectly ugly.

Cooper's, Swainson's, red-tailed, rough-legged, and whatever hawks deny peaceful existences for small savory critters. Cooper's hawks concede the open skies to their larger relatives. Instead, they prefer to dodge and weave through the trees like feathered fighter pilots while looking for unsuspecting sparrows.

When they aren't patrolling the skies on broad wings, the larger hawks resume their surveillance high in the trees. One day, as we passed beneath an angry red-tailed hawk, it flew down from its perch and assaulted Koko. Luckily the bird survived. Years later, Yoshi avenged this insult when she stole a rabbit from its grandchild.

Horned owls only appear when I stand beneath their tree and slowly examine every branch and suspicious knob.

The menu for the alpha predators includes bunnies, squirrels, voles, ducks, and geese. Magpies and crows haggle for table scraps. Kingfishers, herons, egrets, and pelicans dine on fish and anything else that wiggles beneath the water's surface.

White-tailed deer sneak into the Club where they will browse along the swales. Insufficient cover prevents them from residing there, and no one is quite sure where they come from. The predominant risk to their survival is vehicle traffic.

Muskrats and turtles find food and security within the ponds. They appear to avoid predation and live long and happy lives. Some of the painted turtles are the size of frying pans and must be the most ancient residents.

And I don't have the space to describe the entire variety of small tweety birds who flitter around the Club. This would be an extremely large biological dissertation all by itself. Late-spring mornings are filled with robins arguing, chickadees taunting, towhees stuttering, kingbirds pewing, flickers drumming, and little brown birds chirping and warbling about important nonsense.

Beginning in mid-spring, hummingbirds barnstorm the wooded fringes of the upper pond. Apple trees and plum bushes might offer early access to nectar and, later in the summer, the bounty of currants might be hard to ignore.

They also have an appetite for insects that swarm near the ponds. Unlike the aerobatic swallows who dart and weave as they feed, the hummingbirds patiently hover and scan the surrounding airspace for tasty bugs. As soon as a juicy gnat enters their crosshairs, the poor bug is intercepted and consumed in a fraction of a second.

In summary, the Club is a little Animal Kingdom and is the perfect place to unleash the old Canis lupus passions that hide within our domesticated companions.

PART THREE

Even though rabbits are the top prize, the girls' next favorite Club activity is hunting voles. These plump rodents will conceal themselves beneath grass or snow and construct passages, like tiny subways, that become visible when the grass is mowed or the snow thaws. I've only seen them when the girls find them. They resemble fat, fluffy mice with almost no tail. If I ever design fur coats for dolls, I will use vole fur. It's quite luxurious and allows them to remain active throughout the winter.

Both Koko and Yoshi inherited the mouser gene. It must be a combination of smell and sound that betray the vole's hidden location. With minimal hesitation, instinct launches the Shiba toward her discovery. This violence poses a risk to the attacker as well. One time, Koko injured her eye when she pounced into a thorny bush, but this was a temporary injury with a lesson learned.

On the other hand, the Shiba pounce may never include careful consideration. It can happen so suddenly. Like an unconscious hair-trigger that spontaneously realigns their priorities and actions. I'll be on a walk with the family pet trotting by my side and, before I can say this next word, I'm feet away from a savage animal thrusting her nose beneath the snow or grass. For most dogs, this primal switch from pet to predator withered away many generations ago. For the Shiba girls, it was another day at the office.

If the snow is sufficiently deep, the Shiba pounce can completely bury the dog's head while it burrows this way and that with remarkable endurance.

An amusing example of this talent occurred when Yoshi dove into a snowbank where she had detected fresh rodent delight. Then Boo dug in and joined Yoshi in her frozen world. A moment later, the vole emerged above their noses and scampered, quite visibly, over the surface of the snow. The whole time, as the vole skittered away to a safer haven, I tried to enlighten the two headless dogs about the futility of their quest.

The only thing Boo ever pounced on was me. At the

same time, she was an enthusiastic hunter. Whether she was partnered with Koko or Yoshi, the pair of dogs fused into a fierce hunting team. Boo assumed the screaming duty, while the Shiba covered any escape routes. Whenever it came to finishing the task, Boo would leave the remaining business to the Shiba.

Although Boo's hearing prevented her from being a successful pouncer, she would stare intently into the grass if a likely scent drifted past her nose. The Shibas respected her instincts and paid attention when Boo stopped to investigate.

She also stumbled upon a few rabbit burrows while hunting with Yoshi. The rabbits should have protected their young with deeper burrows, but they didn't. Yoshi had no complaints.

Birds, especially goslings and ducklings, have tempted Yoshi's appetite as well. She has learned to avoid them when they're on the water and protected by their parents. But if they're out of the water and foraging in the grass, it's a different game. I have found myself playing momma goose several times as I herded the little guys back into the ponds.

I'm in no position to judge a dog's morality, but I would often interfere to satisfy my own conscience. Each girl came from a lineage that predates our concepts of right and wrong and good and bad. They follow a code of behavior that Man had yet to devise.

Then, as soon as we got back home, the fierce beast vanished and became a lazy dog who never moved until it was time to roll over and get a belly rub—like a mighty hunter returning from a wild adventure before collapsing into a comfy-chair-induced coma.

ROAMING THE AISLES

Leaving Boo at home for extended periods was never an option. Our codependency was clinical. At the same time, I never enjoyed leaving her inside the truck when we went shopping. Over time I found several stores that welcomed the patronage of my four-legged child. Many of these destinations appreciated Boo's lovable spirit and my generous purchases of man-toys and doggy-schlock. A large portion of my income was converted into rawhide and pigs' ears. My only complaint was the suggestive product displays on the lower shelves.

Boo learned to differentiate the friendly stores from the unfriendly. If we were shopping for groceries, she would scrunch down on the passenger seat, frown, and ignore my apologies. But if it was a hardware or sporting goods store, she would jump onto my lap before I could shut the engine off.

Of course, pet stores were my shopping buddy's primary choice. The exotic birds, guinea pigs, ferrets, and lizards provided endless fascination. And these shops also failed to conceal their supply of sparsely wrapped meat bones and dried cow parts.

"Do you want this one?"

"Yarph!"

"And this one?"

"Yarph!"

And so on.

Leashes were often required. But this limitation made it difficult to find my critical supplies in a timely manner. I bought stuff for Boo just to keep moving. She could not travel five feet before the next beguiling item seized her attention.

It wasn't long before I let Boo do her own shopping. This worked until she learned how to operate the automatic entry doors. There were a couple of times when she wandered into the parking lot while searching for me. If not for vigilant store employees, her whereabouts may have remained a mystery. But most of the time she would cruise through the aisles until she befriended a child or similar sucker.

Losing my girl among the aisles of gizmos and gadgets was effortless. Neither of us would be searching for the same thing. Boo followed her nose and I followed my desire for a new overpriced knickknack. We both admired the hardware store's leather gloves and nail pouches for different reasons.

In the middle of the Gander Mountain store, the remains of a large black bear were displayed in a threatening pose that suggested imminent violence. On her first visit to this store, Boo gave the bear a thorough tongue-lashing until it acquiesced with snarling defiance. On subsequent visits, she paid no attention to the mollified beast.

Whenever I lost her in Gander Mountain, the pet supply aisle, with its disingenuous temptations, was a likely detour. The fishy aroma of the live bait section would be the next possibility. And if she wasn't there either, I'd listen for the enthusiastic sound of "Daddy, look! A doggy! My doggy!"

Indeed, for most young children, shopping sucks. Their immature minds cannot appreciate the miracles of credit cards and piles of necessities. Then their trauma vanishes when a tired white dog is discovered in the center of the aisle. Now it's the parent's turn to be disenchanted.

"Let's go, honey."

"No!"

"Mommy's waiting for us."

"No! Can we take him home?"

"That's not our doggy."

"No!"

And so on.

At the big hardware stores, the good lumber is often concealed beneath a deep layer of warped lumber. I have invested a large amount of sweat equity tossing the twisted boards onto the floor and exposing the straight and untouched lumber. As Boo grew older and less adventurous, this project became an excuse for a nap. With her sprawled-out body filling the remaining space across the aisle, she effectively prohibited any interference with our shared endeavor.

Many stores display mandatory food groups such as beef jerky next to the checkout counters. A worthy sporting goods enterprise will place nothing but echelons of beef products at these locations. Boo didn't need a literary degree to know what hid inside these enticing packages.

While she examined the variety of processed meats, a smiling clerk would lean over the counter and distract her with a small dog biscuit. Her usual response was to accept the treat, drop it on the floor, and stare at it with offence. When compared to the array of beefy deliciousness that dangled inches from her nose, a tiny fake dog bone with questionable composition was an insult.

As I completed my purchases, Boo often surveyed the space behind the counter. There had to be something better than a tasteless dog treat. If the clerk didn't notice the entry of her new furry assistant, Boo's rummaging nose would consistently score a startled reaction. Then the clerk would laugh and coo and offer her another suspicious confection.

Her all-time favorite snack did not come from any shop

or store. In fact, I must diverge slightly from the theme of this essay and travel to the corner of Grove Street and Capital Boulevard in Boise. Whenever I visit the Treasure Valley, I never miss the chance to stop at Bar Gernika and enjoy a side of croquettas, a chorizo supreme smothered with pimentos, and one or two beers.

On one of these visits, I poked my head inside the door and waved at Jeff, who was preparing food for his customers. With Boo straining her leash toward the beckoning grill, I told him we would be outside on the patio. Soon our waitress arrived, wrote down my usual order, and was introduced to Boo. While we waited and settled into the ambiance of the Basque Block, Jeff came out to visit and brought a bowl of water for my sidekick.

I shared a few croquettas with my girl, but the chorizo was all mine. This sustenance was necessary for the day ahead. When the waitress arrived with my bill, she placed another small mixing bowl in front of Boo. It was filled with a heap of steaming sliced lamb. Five seconds later, there was nothing left except a mirror finish on the stainless steel. After paying our bill (and, hopefully, leaving a decent gratuity) it was time to say goodbye to my friends. But Boo disagreed and went back to polishing her bowl. I almost had to leave her there.

BACK TO MONTANA

PART ONE

One year after our first vacation, Boo and I returned for another camping trip in the Big Sky Country. We were also pursuing a glorious future in the world of agility, so our first stop was a trial in Billings. With a week's worth of camping supplies and all my agility gear, the only free space in my truck was the front seat.

Convincing the Idaho boys to schedule their time-off around my strange ambitions had made this detour possible. As the sun rose on the first day of the trial, the success of my persuasion came into question.

Before this vacation, I was only familiar with the idyllic summers of western Montana. Billings was different and I was not prepared. With the heat climbing into the nineties, and possibly higher, the agility trial was a surrogate for Hades. For two days, we were captives within the relative comfort of my shade tent.

I wish I could share all the pleasant memories and excellent performances from this trial, but there were none. The second day seemed hotter than the first and I could only think about escaping into higher elevations. With Boo laying at my feet in a melting clump of dirty fur, my collection of maps for the Beartooth Mountains provided settings for my backcountry fantasies.

After completing our lackluster runs and packing up, we had enough time to visit the Yellowstone River before driving to our next destination in the mountains. Between the truck and the river was a long stretch of smooth river rock. As we walked over the stones, Boo yelped in pain and refused to move. I thought she had cut her foot, but there were no obvious injuries. Then I put my hand on a rock that was burning like a hot skillet. Mumbling a string of profanities, I carried her to the river where the cool water brought instant relief. After a brief respite, I picked her up and returned to my truck. This was our only vacation for the year and we were off to a miserable start.

The next leg of our journey took us through Red Lodge and toward Beartooth Pass. Tall mountains engulfed the road until miles of switchbacks put the valley three thousand feet below us. The recent past faded into a distant memory. Boo pushed her nose into the airstream with excited anticipation. Our ascent ended at a plateau of granitic gneiss that was born near the beginning of the Precambrian era. Stunted tundra vegetation clung to the thin soil with determined vigor. This was no longer a fantasy. We were now in the Beartooth Mountains, a neighbor, ecological sibling, and geologic ancestor of Yellowstone National Park.

When we were young, Sara and I spent many summer days at the top of Beartooth Pass. We weren't camping or sightseeing. No, we were skiing down an icy headwall on the north side of the pass. Seeing this place thirty years later created a sensation of déjà vu laced with vertigo. My respect for gravity has grown since my days as a young skier.

A few miles down from the pass, we entered Wyoming and followed a rocky two-track road to a small alpine lake where I had agreed to meet my fellow campers.

When planning summer camping trips, we often select unfamiliar places—wild and isolated destinations with the promise of untold stories. Therefore the initial challenge is to reunite with the Idaho boys without winding up at different predetermined locations (which is possible if specific details are omitted during the planning stage). Only once have we failed in this task.

This time, we had a successful reunion with Tim and Darrin. Tim's dogs Abby and Cliff also greeted us at the lake. And Boo went on guard duty.

We dug into our beer supply and walked down to the shore. Tim grabbed a fist-sized rock and threw it into the freezing water. On cue, Abby dove into the lake before swimming to the bottom. There, she found the rock—or a similar-looking cousin—among the thousands of submerged stones.

The following day, we fished, explored, and found a pile of bear crap that towered above the tundra. This must have come from a grizzly who had a huge posterior and equally large business end and appetite. Wolves may have wandered through this country as well. Then there's Mother Nature who willingly shares her charms before unloading buckets of whoop-ass.

PART TWO

The next morning, we drove to a trailhead at Island Lake for a three-day camping trip in the high country. With my old Kelty frame pack stuffed like a giant cabbage roll, I began my first backpacking trip with Boo.

My hiking style was a slow and steady plod up the trail. This had a Zen-like (or sloth-like) quality. I only paused briefly between every few steps to catch my breath or grab a quick sip of water. Darrin and Tim hiked faster, but their rest stops were longer, so our progress was similar.

Boo's style was to constantly shadow me. As one might

imagine, my boot heels swung into her jaw with unnerving frequency. Each time when I felt the contact and heard her teeth snap shut, I sent her to the front until she eventually circled back into the kicking zone. Sometimes she went exploring with the other dogs then returned and fell in behind me. After less than one mile of hiking, I was forced to shuffle up the trail as if I were wearing my pants around my ankles.

It was a six-mile hike to Albino Lake. The first five-and-a-half miles climbed through Wyoming. The last half-mile climbed higher into Montana. The state line was imaginary and the dimensions of the sky remained the same. A steep gradient at the end added thirty pounds to my pack. My shortened stride contributed another twenty pounds of imaginary gear.

Albino Lake sits above the timberline and finding a suitable place for camping required low expectations. We finally settled on a somewhat-level spot that was protected by a handful of short and scraggly spruce trees. There was a firepit on this small alpine bench, but this was only for decoration. The few trees near the camp had been stripped of their dry tinder and any substantial firewood was miles away.

Tim claimed the sheltered spot near the trees while Darrin and I found two amendable areas among the rocks.

The following morning, we set out to fish Albino Lake. There were exactly zero trout in this lake. The deep cobalt-blue water framed by green tundra and majestic mountains was a waste of scenery. I had fished enough high-country lakes to know when one's dead. Boo and I fished for several hours and not one fish bothered to examine my entire inventory of tempting fuzzy flies. To salvage the experience, I snapped a few photos before hiking down to our camp.

From our campsite, I had a good view of Albino Lake's outlet creek. A short while later, Darrin appeared as he worked his way back along the creek. Like me, he must have abandoned any hope of catching fish. Then he stopped and cast his line into a small pool below a waterfall. Almost immediately, his rod bent toward a splashing resistance on the end of his line. He repeated this performance several times. I assumed he was catching brook trout. Although brookies are common in mountain lakes and streams, they rarely get much larger than a sardine. When Darrin returned to our camp, his stringer of fat cutthroat trout disproved my assumption.

With the fishing gods finally smiling in our favor, Boo and I headed over to the waterfall. I posed like an outdoor magazine cover boy while hauling in one chunky trout after another. The best part of this fish windfall was Boo's eager assistance as each trout came to the shore. She was beginning to understand how slapping water with a stick and string can produce miraculous results—sometimes.

That evening, I prepared a hearty jumping trout stew while we competed in a fish-head-tossing contest. Darrin won the event with a tremendous heave.

Completely uninvited, the storm crashed our party. With an unrelenting downpour filling the air, all six of us crammed our soggy bodies inside Tim's tent and endured a cramped and moist evening. When our supply of fun dwindled into discomfort, we hunkered down inside our own tents.

I don't think Boo ever recovered from this stormy night. Lightning randomly picketed around our exposed location with a constant barrage of violent voltage. As we settled ourselves inside the tent, the surrounding mountainous skyline became visible whenever a flash of lightning lit up the night. And each flash was accompanied by ground-shaking thunder. The fabric of the tent and rainfly vanished for an instant, the earth trembled, then darkness and the sound of rain pelting our fragile shelter returned.

Luckily, every one of those innumerable lightning bolts somehow missed us.

Sunshine has never been more welcome than it was on the following morning when the sun finally climbed above the mountains. Boo was a mess and we cuddled on a sunny rock while absorbing the radiant warmth. After achieving a semblance of life, we broke camp and retreated down the mountain.

The last few miles of our hike to the trailhead were fueled by thoughts of kicking back and guzzling some cold brews. We had left a healthy stash of beer in the back of Tim's truck down at Island Lake. Our plan was to drive back to the rendezvous lake for a final night of camping while working through a case of Henry's.

When we arrived at our trucks, the beer was gone. Our mountain-man machismo instantly deflated into panic and self-pity. A Forest Service note had been placed on Tim's windshield and this informed us about the dangers of beer-guzzling bears. Perhaps we shouldn't have stored our refreshments in the open bed of a truck, but we had tried to conceal them. Unfortunately the rangers were accomplished and dedicated beer detectives.

The better part of a twelve-pack was still stored inside my truck. But it was a paltry concession. Rest would not be possible until our craving for multiple cold brews had been satisfied.

Following the instructions on the Forest Service note,

our precious stash was rescued from the local ranger station. With renewed but weary enthusiasm, we traveled down the mountain highway until a secluded campsite welcomed us for a final night of whatever.

My first beer was nearly empty when the dogs, who had fully recovered from the alpine ordeal, chased after two deer and disappeared into the woods. As we were in another strange and unknown location, I worried about losing Boo. The woods were quite dense and I wasn't sure whether she could find her way back. Searching for a half-deaf dog in an unfamiliar forest might have been difficult.

A few minutes passed before she emerged from the woods. By the look on her face, this may have been the highlight of the entire vacation. The other two-thirds of the pack returned about a minute later. Then we cracked open another beer.

Throughout her life, Boo never lost her bearings. It was uncanny. At the same time, I never became complacent if she disappeared.

When we returned home, Boo slowly recovered from the effects of high-altitude exposure. Her pink eyelids had become crusted over with black mucus, and thin scabs had developed on her nose. As the healing process erased these blemishes, I had fewer misgivings about the Beartooth adventure. And except for the thunderstorm, I doubt she had any regrets.

MAKING PRETTY

Preventing our lovely puppies from wallowing in mud or rolling in dead things might be a good reason for keeping them on a leash. No screaming, yelling, or swearing will steer them away from their filthy destination.

Bathing in mud might offer soothing relief from brutal summer weather. But this must result in a level of discomfort when the mud dries and the dog begins to resemble a Chupacabra. Some humans indulge in this pastime as well. This allure may date back to when we all sprang from the primordial ooze.

Much to their credit, Koko and Boo avoided mud. Sachi avoided any unpleasant habit. Then there's Yoshi, who loves deep pools of mud with the appropriate soupy consistency and full complement of microbes. And she remembers the exact location of each one, so she can return again and again.

During mud season and along the trails of the Cherry Creek dog park, a true aficionado will find irresistible ditches filled with sloppy gumbo. Folks who don't share this enthusiasm will put leashes on their pretty pets when they approach these stretches. Others will shriek and yell and assume this will work. I put myself in the category with those who attempt useless verbal persuasions.

Rolling in dead things and manure distinguishes dogs from other sensible creatures. Young pups will learn this pleasurable activity by pure instinct. Their reason for engaging in this ritual is an ancient mystery. Did their wild ancestors deliberately camouflage themselves as vile and putrid beasts? Is it invigorating? Is it fun? Is it sexy?

Even though the term "roll on" would describe this

recreation, it's more accurate to use "roll in" as it can be a total immersive process.

Like I've said, Koko and Boo were not mud dogs. But if it smelled like pure evil, resistance was futile. For them, mud was filthy and distasteful. But anything that produced a wretched odor was an oasis of happiness. Over the years, their love for this indulgence slowly diminished. Yoshi's struggle is still a matter of concern.

While purposely degrading herself, Yoshi never forgets to include her face. She smears one cheek, then repositions herself before applying a layer of filth on the other side. The only rational explanation is this: there's something very wrong with her.

Once the evil deed is done, you're lucky if there's a good swimming hole nearby (and even more blessed if you have a dog who enjoys swimming). This was a simple process when dealing with Boo. With Koko and Yoshi, I would lure them to the edge of a deep pool and push them into the water. I felt no remorse for this betrayal, but physically touching them was regretful.

And if the water is too shallow, the doggy's enabler must perform the horrible task of grabbing and scrubbing and scrubbing some more. There were a few times when I wished there were a shower nearby—for me.

One day, while fishing along the Smith's Fork River in Wyoming, Tim's dog, Zeke, performed an amazing backflip onto a fresh steaming stew of cow manure.

Like Boo, Zeke was nearly completely white—at least I assumed he was. He often adorned himself with foreign materials. Although he appeared to have a good measure of Aussie or Border Collie, his origins were more mysterious. And he was less protective and more adventurous than Boo.

Prior to Zeke's discovery near the Smith's Fork, the lush forage covering the meadow had been processed into something that resembled five gallons of creamed spinach. His display of gymnastic artistry was embellished with a vigorous backstroke through the pile. I gave it a perfect ten out of ten, but also felt sorry for Tim as he dragged his ebullient green dog to the creek for a power bath. Leaving Tim to his dirty chore, Boo and I headed upstream where the trout lingered in clear and unpolluted water.

Whenever my beautiful girl thoroughly obliterated her attractiveness, effective sanitation would be delayed until I had the proper accessories. The dreaded garden hose was often used for moderate decontamination. Extreme odor required lathering and rinsing. We usually slept with the windows open.

While transporting my former princesses back home, the passenger seat was reserved for cleanliness. Fetid pets were condemned to the back of the truck where my nose would not be offended. Luckily, I could leave a stinky Koko or Yoshi at my mom's house and forget about it. But Boo and her coating of rancid slime were my responsibilities.

Although fresh crap and ripe remnants are good shit, these are not as common as the old dried-up stuff. For a dog, the old stuff is better than nothing. Like summer festival revelers waiting for an available latrine, our lovely pets will eagerly get in line for a chance to roll in some well-aged stink. The remains of skunks and fish can be persistent and captivating for many months. These areas resemble ground zero where the grass has been flattened and some poor old critter has been reduced to parchment.

These well-used rolling zones are great places for developing the perfect rolling technique. Unlike people, dogs don't normally lie on their backs. The exceptions are when they feel submissive, need a belly rub, or find something that's swarming with flies.

To execute a perfect stinky roll, the dog must remain in an inverted position over the target area while aggressively kicking their legs with spasms of joy. This technique, if performed properly, grinds the foul odor deep into the fur on their backs. It's a difficult maneuver and can require multiple attempts until the dog is satisfied with the results.

Sometimes Boo was pampered with a real bath for no specific reason. I couldn't believe how beautiful she could be after a professional scrubbing, drying, and combing. At the same time, I never saw the need for this. I only bathed her when it was a secondary benefit from a short swim.

She couldn't always join me on my adventures. Hunting and ice-fishing trips fit into this category. My only option was to leave her with my mom and this worked quite well. If both of us hit the road for an extended trip, Mom would miss her company, but this was not a serious thing—until Yoshi came into our lives. Then my sister stepped in and offered to relieve Mom's mental distress.

The previous year, before Sara's intervention, Boo and I took a vacation and left Mom with the task of handling Yoshi all by herself. Yoshi was still in her first year but had matured enough to be a tyrant.

Whenever and wherever I could find cell phone service, I would call my mom, give her an update, and wonder how things were going back in Denver. If I bypassed her answering service and made actual contact with Mom, the conversations remained largely one-sided: "When are you coming home? I can't handle this little monster! When are you coming home? She's driving me crazy! WHEN ARE YOU COMING HOME?!"

Thanks to Sara, this was the last time Mom endured Yoshi's wrath. My sister is an angel. She began arranging visits when I abandoned Mom and Yoshi, or left both Boo and Yoshi back in Denver.

Apparently angels have sensitive noses and are skilled at finding local doggy boutiques. Every time when Boo stayed with Sara and Mom, I would return and be greeted by a thoroughly washed and groomed calendar girl who dazzled me with whiteness. A lovely fabric flower always decorated her collar and she smelled like a bed of roses.

Then we went out to find something to roll in.

HEAVY WEATHER

Winter snowstorms will always remind me of Boo. Even without her company, I may wander into the night whenever it snows. The deeper the snow, the more I feel her presence.

Less than one year after Boo's spirit returned to heaven and during the second snowstorm of the season, I performed the ritual of lacing up my boots, wrapping a scarf around my neck, insulating my torso with a thick layer of wool, and pulling a cap and gloves over my extremities. Then I stepped into a snowy nighttime world and closed the door behind me.

Enough snow had fallen to erase most of the darkness. As I trudged across the golf course, all available light was consumed by infinite reflections within a glowing tinted landscape. Aside from a hint of smoldering hardwood, the air was cold and clean. My consciousness was sharp and invigorated. I walked to the top of a sand trap on the sixteenth fairway to view the muted city lights below me and observe the silence.

There's a haggard Russian olive tree next to the sand trap. A great horned owl would perch on this tortured snag and solemnly wait for a rabbit to appear. His presence never met Boo's approval and she would admonish him until he flew away. He was not there on this night. Nor had any other souls shared my inclination. I was alone with a company of memories.

Behind me, a solitary set of tracks led to where I stood. To my left was a blanket of snow where the tracks would follow me back home.

I've already recounted a few stories where inclement weather was a key factor. In all honesty, light rain showers and snowstorms were preferred conditions. While accepting a bearable amount of discomfort, these storms minimized conflicts with animal control officers and other authorities of civil behavior. Of course, hailstorms and thunderstorms were avoided whenever possible.

Dogs love snow. This is an undeniable fact. So why does the number of dedicated dog lovers shrink into a few brave and frumpy souls on cold and snowy days? I'm not sure. It's likely their neglected companions, who are stuck at home on these days, complain loudly and piddle on the family room rug.

Extremely cold days—as in single-digit and below-zero days—can hobble dogs as the frost burns into their feet. Those with youth and energy might overcome this affliction. For my older girls, it was often necessary to shed my gloves and warm their paws before carrying them back to the car.

Younger pups carelessly porpoise through deep drifts of snow as if they were dancing in the clouds. Older dogs stay grounded and follow established trails. My warmth comes from maintaining these trails. Regardless of the dog's age, these arctic intrusions will stir the fire in their souls. This is the benefit of braving the elements: the pure satisfaction of thorough exhaustion.

Sometimes I would dust off my cross-country skis to pay homage to my Scandinavian ancestry. Don't try this. Our rambunctious sidekicks will never appreciate the delicate balance and skill that are required for this sport. And once you are reduced into a tangle of ski gear, paws, and tongues, the true test of Nordic proficiency will begin.

During my first winter with Boo, we drove to the Cherry Creek dog park to kick-start another day. A storm had moved in overnight and the snow was blowing sideways. There was no cover to absorb the driving force of the blizzard. With the storm pushing us forward, we forged a path into the open fields on the south end of the park.

For half an hour, we made good progress. Then it was time to loop back to the truck and push our faces into the stinging ice crystals. My eyeglasses became coated with ice. It was like looking at a white wall through a bubble-wrap window. I couldn't see anything, let alone a white dog. My visual range was reduced to less than two hundred feet and the storm was devouring all sound.

I assume Boo was having a similar problem and we became separated. Although she was familiar with the park, the landscape had been transformed into layers of white-noise. This was back when coyotes were quite prevalent in these fields. Perhaps one or more coyotes had drawn her away from me; I'll never know. If Boo had detected their presence, her angry barks and screams might have pierced the howling silence. With her inability to follow the sound of my voice, I stayed silent while my heart pounded.

I finally came upon another person whose priorities had led him into this raging blizzard. Although he was concerned about my predicament, he was unable to help. As my energy and ideas ran low, I gave up searching. Maybe she had found her way back to the parking lot.

And sure enough, after slogging half a mile to my truck, I nearly cried with relief as my tension evaporated. When I waved my arms and shouted her name, Boo jumped to her feet, raced toward me, launched all four paws into my chest, and almost knocked me over.

Serious rainstorms and wet snow are not fun for people or dogs. Everyone and everything gets cold and soaked. If it was a bad storm, the girls would pause frequently and shake their saturated coats. Somehow this incessant shaking, with body parts flying in opposite directions, never dislocated any limbs or tails. Assuming lightning was not a threat, we always plunged into downpours of rain and wet snow to address the demands of nature.

A dog's ability to shake water from its fur is based on a cascading series of fast-twitch oscillations. It's a skill all pups master at a young age and gradually lose as they get older. It starts with a slow shake of the head. This gentle cadence then accelerates and travels down the spine until it becomes a doggy spin cycle. Anything within five feet gets a free shower.

Boo always performed her final shake on the passenger seat. Even though I dried her with a towel outside the truck, this was never sufficient. So, in addition to a thorough toweling, I taught her how to shake before jumping into the truck. This lesson included the command "shake" and swinging my head from side to side as a poor demonstration. She would comply with my awkward demand, climb onto her seat, and spray my dashboard and windows with any remaining moisture.

There were several times when an ominous storm was filling the sky and we attempted to complete our walk before it hit. This was hopeful thinking. Storms will never show any concern for the schedules of people and their pets.

One afternoon, Boo, Sachi, and I were finishing another expedition around the Club. The parking area was less than a hundred yards up the trail. There was a good chance we could beat the oncoming storm. Then, I heard a crackling sound and saw sparks flying from the top of a pine tree about fifty feet away. It was like a natural fireworks display. My first thought was, "Wow! That's cool!"

This reaction was followed by a small nugget of reason. The firecracker tree may have been a preamble to a lightning strike. Charged electrons were searching for something to fry. While considering this wisdom, lightning exploded near the parking area. It was tangible but not fatal. They say lightning never strikes twice, so we ran to my truck and avoided electrocution.

I've never found a good explanation for this terrifying experience. We've witnessed many unexplained things while exploring nature. God's design can be very elusive when I'm searching for an answer. And when least expected, these mysteries can produce an impressive pucker factor.

The sparkling tree incident, the Beartooth nightmare, the Dumb Friends' parking lot drama, and other conflicts with darkened skies instilled an absolute fear of thunder within Boo's psyche. Her logic was more precise than mine.

Despite her hearing impairment, she could detect faraway thunder like a finely tuned seismograph. Then she trembled with fear. The roles we had been assigned were awkwardly reversed as I ran my hand along her back and consoled her with nonsense until the storm finally relented.

The heavy thunderstorms of the Front Range resulted in many long nights when I used my parental powers to bring calm to my frightened girl. After an abbreviated night of rest, we'd wake up, go outside to pee, and everything was good again.

CHERRY CREEK

PART ONE

My townhouse huddles among others near the top of a gentle suburban ridge. Commanding views of the Front Range metropolitan expanse can be found within this settlement. It's an effective defensive position should the Urbanites challenge our sovereign territory.

Every July Fourth, we watched numerous fireworks flashing over the Platte River Valley like fairyland ordnance. But this was never fun for Boo, who hated the Fourth. Her torture began a few weeks before the holiday and lasted a few weeks after, until the local supply of black powder was finally extinguished for the year.

Cherry Creek lies to the west of this ridge and Tollgate Creek is the eastern boundary. Although Cherry Creek can shrink into a series of disconnected pools during long, hot summers, it's a respectable tributary to the South Platte River. As a historical note, before Colorado became a state, one of the first gold strikes in the Kansas Territory was along Cherry Creek.

The first local beer may have come from Cherry Creek as well. I've found no documentation to support this, but it could be true. The area around Cherry Creek State Park has an abundance of wild rye. Not far from this ryegrass, feral hops drape themselves over surrounding vegetation. And there are several springs along the creek that would provide clean, untainted water. This smells like beer to me—with a hint of good rye whiskey.

And it must be an ancient creek. There's a stretch along

the creek called "Fossil Beach" where the girls swam and waded while I prospected. Pieces of fractured petrified wood are scattered among the cobbles. Some of these ancient tree relicts, which resemble flint, display sculpted edges like stone-age hardware.

It's easy to imagine a prehistoric landscape where huge short-faced bears and saber-toothed cats frolicked in the creek with giant bison and woolly mammoths, while trendy fur-clad Denverites badgered them with stone weapons.

The respect for this little creek (and for whomever held claims to its water) is evident where Cherry Creek crosses the High Line Canal. This canal was built in the late 1800s to transport water from the South Platte and into the thirsty Piedmont. To maintain a proper grade for the canal, it follows a lengthy sinuous course across the hills and valleys of the Piedmont. Minor watercourses were severed and larger ones required some consideration.

When the canal's construction reached Cherry Creek, a wooden flume was fabricated to carry the canal's water over the creek. This bypass was upgraded to an underground concrete siphon in the 1930s. The siphon swallows the canal water on one side of the creek, then spits it out on the other side. It's a fascinating diversion that created a waterfall where the creek passes over the siphon and plunges (or dribbles) into a doggy swimming hole.

A couple of decades after the canal's siphon had been completed, and a few miles to the south, the Army Corps of Engineers tamed the feisty creek with a hundred-and-forty-foot dam that spread nearly three miles across the valley. Behind Cherry Creek Dam, the creek swelled to a notable size and various watercraft began to paddle, row, sail, and motor across its surface.

Despite this impressive obstruction—and despite the establishment of a generous, but restrained channel within Denver—Cherry Creek remains relatively free as it playfully gurgles toward the skyscrapers of Downtown. In fact, Denver was originally founded at the confluence of Cherry Creek and the South Platte River.

Cherry Creek Dam is spitting distance from my home. Not only does it provide flood control, but it also divides the creek into two personalities: the lower creek, which drains from the lake, and the upper creek, which fills the lake. Places where dogs can run wild and free are limited on the lower creek. This stretch is more metropolitan and home to ill-tempered coyotes and bicyclists.

At the same time, the lower creek offers deeper pockets of water. For Boo, some of these were large enough for a short swim. This is where Yoshi learned her aquatic talents. Koko and Sachi would let the cool, lazy water rise above their bellies with big smiles spread across their faces.

Above the lake, and inside the state park, the upper creek offers more acreage for adventure and fewer coyote and biker conflicts.

The upper creek can be further defined by three distinct communities: the forest, the swamp, and the sandy creek. Within the state park, the forest and swamp are off-limits to free-roaming pets. In other words, this forbidden realm became our private refuge.

The forest is primarily a cottonwood forest with black willow trees growing along the creek. The landscape is mired in a savage era. Beneath the canopy, the musty odor of woody decay often hangs in the air. Deadfall limbs and logs litter the ground like oversized pick-up-sticks. Uprooted and beaver-gnawed cottonwoods straddle the creek at irregular intervals. Black willows collapse and repopulate as their branches become new trees. An abundance of leaners and widow-makers requires constant vigilance, especially on windy days.

Within the forest, the creek digs a deep, winding gully until it spills into the lake. It cuts straight down through soft soil and largely forbids access to its channel. Deep fishable pools form along the bends. A size-eight Eagle Claw fishhook dressed with a fat nightcrawler can be quite effective on trout, carp, wipers, and bullheads.

The girls and I followed deer trails and lightly used paths through the forest. It was unusual to see other people and even more unusual to see another dog. Primitive shelters made from local and imported materials suggested a need for seclusion deep inside the woods. We never saw the folks who inhabited these patchwork homes, but we also never bothered to conduct a closer investigation.

At one time, while tracing the bones of an abandoned railroad, West Cherry Creek Road passed nearby and into the town of Melvin. Then the road turned east and traversed the forest before connecting with East Cherry Creek Road (also known as Parker Road). After years of neglect, the western road became another phantom within the state park's wilderness. The town of Melvin itself was removed from local maps and transformed into a shooting range within the state park. On a happier note, some industrious historians preserved the Melvin schoolhouse, and it was relocated to the Smokey Hill High School campus.

As the old road to Melvin wasted away, it created a dam across Cherry Creek. A cattail swamp filled the flooded upstream side. This is where the swamp begins. My trips into this sloppy ecosystem have been limited by claustrophobia.

Boo was more familiar with its dank interior.

Coyotes have dens deep inside the swamp. Their domain is defended by a tangled barrier of willows, currants, and thatched cattails. Small openings along the edge create portals for their daily commutes.

When Boo was young and fearless, she would venture through the portals and into the hidden coyote corridors. There was no way I could have followed her and any rescue would have been a mess. After burrowing into the coyotes' quagmire, she would issue a bellicose challenge to announce her arrival. Her continuous ranting combined with quivering cattail stalks provided the only clues for her whereabouts. Even though she never became disoriented, stuck, or injured, it was never entertaining.

There is also a small, obscure parcel where the forest and swamp merge and create swampy timber. This is a good place to observe mycological wonders sprouting from the cottonwoods and willows.

Boo and I often wallowed through the swampy timber for personal reasons. Black rancid mud would engulf the lower portions of our bodies while dead tree branches clawed at our faces. If I expected an extensive slog through deep muck, I would bring a change of clothes to avoid offending any civilized folks whom we might encounter on our way out.

Although I've referred to it as "mud," it's more like a viscous stew of decaying matter that's been spoiling for many years. As a result, Boo became a black, smelly swamp thing. I would address this issue by throwing a stick into a channel where the water ran deep and clear. This worked fairly well and resulted in a near-white dog with a rank odor that persisted for a few more days.

PART TWO

The upstream edge of the Cherry Creek swamp is the western border of the dog park. This is where solitude ends and where doggy people and people doggies run wild and unleashed. This dog park is nearly a hundred acres of open space and resembles a high-desert grassland, with bunch grasses, wild plums, lupins, Spanish bayonets, rabbit brush, prickly pear cacti, and sundry weeds. Cottonwoods and black willows continue to thrive along the banks of the creek.

Within this gritty and arid terrain, the creek flows over a bed of sand and gravel and the water can be crystal clear. I call this the sandy creek stretch. If it's flooding or hosting a doggy convention, the water can appear less pristine.

Shallow Denver Basin aquifers contribute to the water's flow and clarity. Within the dog park, a large spring fills a popular doggy swimming hole. Even though the water can appear to be potable, the risk of Shih Tzu contamination should be considered.

This stretch of Cherry Creek is ideal for people and their canine masters. Its presence consummates the best dog park in the Denver area.

On warm summer days, the dog park's sandy creek resembles a doggy Woodstock, with happy puppies playing, splashing, lying down, and peeing in the creek. Except for a deeper pool of water near the big spring, the water is rarely above my ankles, and the creek itself is a thoroughfare for people and their pups. Large migrations of tennis balls can be observed as they swim downstream to their breeding ground. Only a few will survive the gauntlet of doggy jaws before spawning the next generation of cheap puppy toys.

Yoshi was a young pup when the state began a major overhaul of the dog park. A large fenced-in area was being constructed, with fences defining the eastern, western, and northern boundaries. The boundary along Cherry Creek, which has always defined the southern extent of this pup playground, would remain unfenced. During the renovation project, upgrades were also being developed along the creek and a temporary fence denied access to its water.

The cheap plastic fence wasn't a deterrent for Yoshi. If there wasn't a hole in it, she knew she could make one. When she was done, the hole was just big enough for her. Luckily, the loaders, graders, and trucks had taken the day off. I expanded the hole for Boo and climbed over the top to chase after Yoshi.

We found her sitting on her favorite beach. She was quite pleased with her adventure and wore a triumphant expression. The little imp was convinced she deserved this special privilege. Fences and warning signs were only necessary for other doggies.

The hole in the temporary fence was never repaired and Yoshi never forgot where it was. If we took detours to avoid the fence hole, Boo would be more obedient and stay with me. I could have kept Yoshi on a leash, but this might have suggested she was disobedient.

There are times when the creek becomes a flooding monster. Cherry Creek drains a large area of the Piedmont that extends to the Palmer Divide. Healthy storms pass over this watershed and dump rain or snow. This dispersed volume of water coalesces and funnels through the state park where the power of these floods can change everything except the creek's name.

To preserve its channel through the dog park, large

boulders were placed along the creek. A flood would bury these with a load of sand. Then a subsequent storm would scour the sand away. One notable gully-washer deviated from the main channel and ripped through a pond that had been a favorite hangout for Boo and her friends. When the torrent subsided, the pond became a beach and was filled with a hundred tons of sand and gravel.

These floods can create dangerous situations for people and their pets. Following several days of heavy rain, Yoshi raced ahead of us and disappeared below a steep bank above the creek. I prayed she wouldn't do anything stupid. My prayers were answered when I looked across the creek and saw Miss Aqua-dog standing on the far bank. She must have been looking for her favorite beach—which was now under three feet of fast-flowing water—and kept paddling until her paws found terra firma. After mindlessly traversing the swollen creek, the dumbstruck Shiba showed no interest in returning to our side.

With my legs submerged in turbulent water, I crossed over to rescue Yoshi. As I expected, Boo followed me, but the flood carried her farther downstream. When Boo finally found us, I grabbed Yoshi and slogged back across. Once again, Boo took the long route before coming ashore somewhere downstream.

While we continued our walk, I debated the wisdom of my amphibious Shiba experiments. Whether it was good or bad, I had already crossed this creek and there was no swimming back.

Once the upgrades were finished, twenty acres on the southwest side of the dog park were excluded and became a no-doggies land. This was where a dry peninsula pushed into the swamp. It was almost as wild as the swamp and the forest. Not many folks explored the peninsula, but there was enough traffic to maintain a few trails.

Multiple creek channels weaved across this hidden retreat and it almost resembled a delta. While most of these were dry, each one was available to become Cherry Creek. Gravelly soil and swaths of deep sand covered the drier areas. Buckwheat, burdocks, currants, and willows bordered each possible channel.

On the south side of the peninsula, beavers maintained a pond that was fed by another spring. Bleached cottonwood timbers within the pond welcomed gatherings of gangly blue herons who sang like they were coughing-up stubborn furballs. If the creek vanished beneath the sand during the summer, this became a reliable swimming hole for Boo, Sachi, and Koko. The flooded forest offered a convenient training opportunity as I guided Boo around the trees and toward her toy.

One morning, while following Boo and Koko across the peninsula, I dialed into a conference call with my East Coast clients. Not long after introducing ourselves, hundreds of geese began rising from the swamp. Each goose had her own opinion and shared it with the others.

I cupped my hand over the phone.

"What's that noise? We can't hear you."

"What? I think we have a bad connection."

"Can you put your phone on mute?"

"One second."

"Thanks, much better."

SNOWY RANGE AGILITY CAMP

During the third year of my descent into agility madness, Boo and I traveled to Laramie for another event. With a national forest looming not far to the west, I decided to camp in the Snowy Range while attending the trial. This added nearly an hour of travel to and from the venue, but an opportunity to combine my passions for camping and doggy sports could not be ignored. At the south end of Laramie, we turned onto Highway 130 and drove toward the distant hills.

Before leaving Aurora, I had reviewed several maps of the area and found a forest road that led to a remote creek near the base of the range. On paper, the location looked perfect, so this became our destination.

After passing through Centennial, we found the forest road and, with half a dog remaining inside the truck, followed it across wooded hillsides. As we approached the creek, it appeared fortune had smiled upon us. The campsite looked ideal. I grabbed my fly rod and walked down to the creek where Boo was already paddling around and chasing surface dimples made by small brook trout. She was in full agreement with my assessment.

The brookies compensated for their tiny stature by eagerly attacking my flies—even with my girl acting like a big white otter. The fishing soon distracted me and I didn't notice Boo's departure. Shifting my eyes upstream, I spotted her among some low-lying willows. Her head was down and she was enjoying a nose-full of something. As long as she was within my sight, I had no reason to interrupt her investigation.

With my preliminary fishing assessment completed—

and while contemplating trout recipes—I returned to my truck and began unloading our gear. Meanwhile Boo was still doing whatever she was doing. She was stubbornly fixated on something. Curiosity prevailed; I had to see if Boo's discovery was worthy of my adulation as well. What I found was an enormous dead beaver that had been there long enough to increase its enormity. My satisfaction imploded and I disregarded my favorable conclusions. I couldn't bury the bloated carcass or throw it in the water. Instead, with this tempting mass of bear bait providing nothing but trouble, we abandoned the perfect camp.

Daylight was becoming a limiting factor.

There was a Forest Service campground farther up the main road and I had briefly visited this campground during previous trips through the Snowy Range. It held the promise of alpine lake fishing and the possibility of less privacy. For some unknown official reason, the campground was closed.

Plan C included aimlessly driving around forest roads and hoping we could find something before nightfall. With amazing foresight, the Forest Service had identified all other campsites and had blocked access to these with large boulders. We finally came upon a spot where an industrious camper had rolled one of the boulders aside. The gap was narrow, but my truck slipped through without any damage. Having witnessed the mighty efforts of the Forest Service, I feared the large block of granite might be rolled back into the barricade while we slept. But I had no choice, there was no Plan D.

The next day, the rock passageway was still open and we drove down to the USDAA agility event in Laramie. There would be some high-caliber competitors and a nationally recognized judge at this event. I was hoping to achieve a little national recognition as well.

That's it. Nothing more to say. Boo performed horribly. She thought we were going fishing and wound up staring into a dusty fieldhouse from the confinement of her crate.

By late afternoon, we were back at our mountain lair and preparing to search for a pond that was a quarter of a mile above our camp. Although there wasn't a trail to the lake, I had a map and a notion of its approximate location. With the wasted hours of the day falling behind us, Boo reclaimed her joyful spirit as she loped across sunny alpine slopes.

Once again, we found small, but willing brook trout. The pond was our private fishing hole until three large and swarthy fishermen showed up. Black tattoos darkened their intentions. We exchanged a silent greeting as they defiantly stomped toward us. Boo was also unusually shy about their presence. When they passed by, I wondered if their ultra-light fishing rods could be weaponized. I knew they had knives. No respectable angler goes fishing without a knife.

Like I said, there was no trail, but somehow, these assumed penitentiary parolees had found our pond. After threatening us with nothing, they plodded along the shore until stopping on the far side. Then they began casting lethal lures into the water.

Boo and I remained on our side and fished for another hour before departing in a direction that led away from our camp. We maintained our deception until we were beyond the felonious eyes of the brotherhood, then scooted back to my truck, ate a quick dinner, and remained vigilant. Moving our camp wasn't an option. Our extensive reconnaissance during the previous evening had confirmed this fact.

As the sun slipped behind the rocky peaks, cold air

descended and settled upon our camp. I pulled a pink sweater over Boo's head and guided her forelegs through the shortened sleeves. This was a test run for a child's sweater that had been modified to fit her body. It accentuated her whiteness and she looked so pretty. As soon as she was properly bundled up, she trotted into a clump of spruce trees and disappeared. Then she emerged from the shadow of the trees and was as naked as the day she was born. Her sweater was gone. There was no reason to look for it.

The next morning, still alive and unmolested, we drove down to the second day of the agility trial. That's all I need to say about this catastrophe. I was upset until I accepted my responsibility. It was a valuable lesson and I gradually recovered from my dog training insanity. At least that's what Boo told me.

And when the Archangel Brethren of the Snowy Range came upon a small pink sweater covered with white dog fur and entangled within the low branches of a wind-blasted spruce tree, they knew they had underestimated the cunning of their adversaries.

SLEEPING ARRANGEMENTS

When Boo first came into my life, I was a single guy who slept, quite contently, in a twin bed. That was all I needed. And that was all Boo needed—provided I didn't intend to share the bed with her.

She was barely thirty-five pounds and I was pushing somewhere over two hundred. Why her claim for bedspace was larger than mine was an enigma. How she managed to push me to the edge was even more puzzling. And somehow, she acquired my spot next to the open window. But I adapted.

To minimize her ownership, I would forcefully flop onto my side of the bed and gain a few additional inches.

While she slept, Boo became extremely animated with dreams about abundant bunnies and truculent coyotes. Her kicking, yelping, and growling portrayed furious surreal adventures. One night I was awakened by a haunting wolf howl. Boo never howled. She must have been taken back to a wonderful primeval wilderness where she harmonized with her pack while hunting plump lagomorphs and mighty ungulates.

When the real coyotes started yipping and howling into the night, Boo could not sleep. Instead, she stood on the bed with her hackles flared and whimpered with rage as she pressed her face into the window screen.

Thunderstorms and fireworks also disrupted Boo's tranquility. She became an agitated mess of trembling and heavy panting. Sleep was impossible for both of us whenever this happened. It was like sleeping with a furry jackhammer.

Although I hated doing this, there were a few times when I moved her onto the doggy bed. In fact, she never objected to this brief exile. I may have been an annoying sleeper as well. If both of us were having a rough time, I would lie on the floor next to her bed while she assumed her role as my therapist. She was very good at understanding the petty dramas in my life.

People food had a bad effect on her digestion. Not long after adopting Boo, I was fast asleep while the consequence of sharing my dinner was churning in her bowels. She slipped down the stairs and settled her business by the door that opened onto my backyard. The next day, I discovered this obvious hint. The only solution was a dog door and a backyard that would be more practical for her needs. Of course, there was the option of not sharing my food, but this would have been cruel.

At that time, my "backyard" was a rotted wood deck and not suitable for my girl. Two months later, Boo had her own doggy door. Her new door led into a doghouse with a second door that opened onto the world's smallest "lawn." I had also constructed two large planters where she could replace my vegetables with chew toys and meat bones.

With the possibility of nighttime accidents minimized, I graduated to a queen bed, where I was allowed one-third of the bed; Boo controlled the remainder. I still own my one-third of this bed. It has been a hard habit to break.

Camping trips brought us back to the good old days of being crammed together. This time, our bed was the back of my truck. It started as an assortment of yoga mats and doggy mattresses, and ended with the taco bed.

The bed of my truck was covered with a topper shell that worked quite well for road camping. After removing my camping supplies and installing the taco bed, my truck was transformed into a small cozy camper.

The taco bed was a large piece of yellow foam that was six inches deep. Prior to being the ultimate camping luxury, it had been used in a high-jump pit at the Kent School. When the school renovated the pit, the old foam was tossed into a garbage pile where I rescued it for a more noble purpose. Instead of trimming the foam to fit my truck bed, I allowed it to curl up the sides and over the wheel wells. It was a sprawling yellow crash pad. My buddies thought we looked like a man-dog taco, so it became the taco bed.

Boo was born with a pink nose and never appreciated the indignity of having sunscreen rubbed on it every day. At the same time, she loved sunscreen when it was on my face. For some reason, the taste of sun lotion combined with sweaty camping grime was irresistible.

When she snuggled next to me in the taco bed, she would lick my ear, wash one side of my face, go back to scrubbing the inner cavity of my ear, and resume bathing my face until I rolled over. Then she worked on the back of my neck and tackled the ear and jowls she had missed previously. She could also insert a large portion of her tongue up my nose. It was like an alien creature was invading my skull. Boo was an extremely thorough face-cleaner.

The best solution was to leave the topper hatch open. This stimulated her guard-dog instincts and she would shift her head away from my tasty face and toward the opening. The proximity of her other end was a concession I had to live with.

But if the chill became excessive or nighttime intruders invaded my imagination, the hatch would be closed and facial time would resume.

Several camping trips with Tim and Darrin included the relative luxury of Forest Service cabins. All these cabins have twin beds as either single beds or, more commonly, as bunk beds. Every mattress is enshrouded with plastic to provide sanitary tackiness.

The dogs often selected their sleeping spots before we began unpacking our supplies. If the cabin only had bunk beds, they would choose the lower bunks. When retiring for the evening, I would squeeze my body between the edge of the mattress and Boo. The upper bunks were never an option. These were used for storage or occupied by Darrin.

Boo's dominion became the bed, along with the zone where I had randomly dumped my shoes, clothes, and whatnots. The other dogs learned to respect this perimeter. To limit any expansion of her domain, I often fed her in the bed. She was a true camping princess.

During our vacation at the Scaler Cabin in Wyoming, we engaged in an unconscious battle for space on the narrow lower bunk. As a result, with her paws pointing toward the ceiling, Boo became stuck between the bed and the wall of the cabin. I don't know how long she was stranded there, but it might have been several hours before I woke up and found her. Boo's stoicism was worthy of sainthood and she never complained about the inconvenience.

Tim, who would not be described as a small man, would squeeze between two dogs while sleeping in a Forest Service twin bed. It was one large mass of dogs and human that defied all known laws of physics.

WINDING IN THE WILLOWS

Any outdoorsman who has tossed a fishing lure into a Rocky Mountain stream is familiar with seamless groves of willows. The act of getting to the stream through densely interwoven branches can be treacherous and sometimes disorienting. Beavers dig deep invisible gullies within this villainous vegetation. These are discovered when one leg disappears into the earth.

Welcome to nature's revenge.

Sometimes cattle will range through the willows and create passable corridors. These cow-trails work better for dogs and other four-legged animals. Two-legged critters like me must crouch or crawl to follow these paths. And if one attempts to carry a fishing pole, he will exhaust his entire wealth of spicy slander.

To limit the abuse, we would often follow a shortcut, only to learn that shortcuts through willows are mythical things. It's common knowledge that trolls and gnomes deliberately engineer these dead-end atrocities.

But a true fisherman will never abandon his quixotic mission.

It was somewhere in Wyoming. I've forgotten the exact location—the stifling interior of a throng of willows allows no geographic certainty. With Boo trailing behind me, we plunged into the wicked gauntlet with herculean aspirations. Branches bent forward by my exertions became spring-loaded switches. It was a constant battle against a pestilence of thwackers. She might have abandoned me, but her loyalty could often be measured by the degree of my insanity.

Success wasn't guaranteed, but the odds for finding no

water were worse. No water means no willows. It's a yin-yang thing. When the sparkling stream finally flowed before us like a dreamy postcard, the nightmare returned as the evil presence encircled us with a profusion of scrawny limbs. The ordeal knew no end.

As soon as Boo finished her swim through my fishing hole, I began working on my back cast. This required several practice casts and a similar number of trips into the willows for retrieving my fly or untangling my line. After twenty or so back casts, I was ready for recreation before delivering my lure into the brush on the far bank.

While my brutal treatment of the encroaching foliage might have been amusing for some folks, it wasn't for Boo. Her concern for my mental health faded and she evaluated other options. Knowing that Tim was somewhere in the same zip code, she set off to track him down. Upon noticing her absence, my brief victory became a search for Tim as well. When I found him, my girl was resting nearby on a grassy bank.

Boo liked Tim. He didn't fuss about obedience. She always enjoyed his mellow company around camp or along a stream. And I had no objections to their tryst. If she disappeared, she was probably tracking the scent of hand-rolled tobacco.

There were other days when neither Tim nor I could account for Boo's presence. She could have been anywhere under the willows. Although calling her back to me wasn't the best option, I would force myself to use a calm normal voice and avoid my preference for scream therapy. Somehow she always found her way back. Then, after a flurry of kisses and butt wiggling, she would share a few minutes of her time before wandering off to find Tim.

At the start of this essay, I alluded to an industrious rodent known as the beaver. In fact, this diabolical critter is responsible for creating and nurturing a bounty of willow monstrosities. Mother Nature gave us beautiful mountains, enchanting creeks, and a few willows. The beaver gave us dam nation. His inability to accept natural order is only exceeded by folks who develop trendy resorts and theme parks.

Beaver dams clog entire valleys and fill them with tons of soil, nutrients, and water. In other words, they build willow-topias. When viewed from above, these plantations resemble giant scouring pads studded with dark sinister ponds. On closer examination, the beaver dams and lodges become defensive ramparts. These fortifications strongly discourage all solicitors with solid walls of treacherous wooden daggers.

And why are beaver houses called lodges? Well, here's why. It's more than just a house; it's a secure retreat where beady-eyed villains plan elaborate inundations.

When gazing upon one of these unsanctioned land-grab developments, an unaware angler might see deep pockets of water and massive hungry trout. In his feverish imagination, the dam is a bridge and the lodge is a casting platform. If luck and determination allow him to reach his destination, his fantasy will quickly unravel—unless his only objective was to constantly untangle fishing line from a jumble of thatched sticks. While he contemplates his misery there will be nowhere to sit. His dog will learn her lessons long before he will.

We inflicted this torture upon ourselves only twice.

To be honest, whenever I fished with Boo, the willows were avoided as much as possible. We often ignored miles of prime fishing water.

One summer day, while fishing on Hobble Creek in Wyoming, the fish refused to cooperate in a forested section of the stream. Boo and I scrambled up a sagebrush hillside to see if the upstream water offered better opportunities. The broad valley was beautiful and enticing as the creek wound through a hideous mass of willows and ponds. Like a hungry trout being drawn to a tempting lure, the illusion was too real to ignore. With minimal hesitation, we descended to where the creek emerged from acres of dense shrubbery and waded into the unknown.

It wasn't long before our progress ended at an old and narrow beaver pond with a thick snaggle of overhanging branches. My first, second, and third casts hit their targets and became embedded in the bushes guarding the pond. The deep water forbade any chance for retrieving my flies. It looked like another dead-end.

Apparently other critters had faced this same issue and we found a well-used game trail. I figured my luck was changing and we had come upon an honest shortcut. This naivety lasted until I saw fresh bear tracks in a muddy stretch of the narrow corridor.

I doubt we were near any bears. During previous wilderness trips, Boo had developed a nose for bear. If one were nearby, her alarm would have disrupted the quiet valley. But with a limited range of visibility, I didn't want to test my theory, so we turned back and fished the barren section of the creek. It was a fruitless day of fishing, but Boo didn't care. Exploring the wild, swimming in the creek, and sniffing and rolling had made it a great day.

There's a sidebar to this story that is near but beyond the realm of the willow. Camping beneath spruce trees is also a bad idea. Tall spruce trees provided welcomed shade at the Hobble Creek camp. Whenever the dogs rested below the spruce boughs, their fur became infested with tar-balls. Pitch oozes from these trees like a sweaty fisherman battling willows under a midsummer sun. Sticky gobs of pitch fall to the ground where they accumulate dirt and debris and are transformed into camouflaged tar-balls. Their presence will be confirmed when they begin to glom onto shoes and pets.

I used a handful of alcohol-infused first aid patches and removed one-and-a-half tar-balls from Boo's coat—about one-tenth of her inventory. My next decision was difficult. After sacrificing a full evening's ration of high-test rum, I removed the remaining tar-balls. There was one drawback to this Black Seal solution: Boo smelled like a rummy for another few days.

Native Americans might have thousands of uses for willows (and spruce trees), but I only have a couple. On a hot day, they might be the only source of shade, and their dead branches are easily converted into a dog toy.

RIDING SHOTGUN

Boo always rode shotgun. If the passenger side was already occupied, her claim was still valid. For myself, I have miles of experience as a Bark-O-Lounger while riding in Tim's truck and jostling along rough Forest Service roads. I was nothing more than a convenient platform as Boo thrust her face into the breeze and anchored her paws upon my thighs. At the end of these trips, my quads were thoroughly tenderized and ready for the skillet.

I accepted full responsibility. The fostering of this behavior began on our first day together. If I was traveling with two dogs, Boo would claim the window seat. Her right to observe passing scenery and enjoy brisk ventilation was not negotiable. And if another human joined us for a ride, I would politely offer them a towel to put on their lap. Although she wasn't a lap dog, a pair of meaty thighs nestled below her window was an open invitation. To discourage this behavior, I created a cozy nest behind the front seats. This was a waste of time and interior design.

To be honest, the passenger seat was her second choice. From the beginning of our relationship, she preferred the driver's seat. This was how she trained me to offer a treat before she would move to the other side.

Having Boo beside me was useful during occasional—and alleged—traffic violations. Her ability to climb onto my lap and schmooze with patrolmen may have resulted in less severe penalties. Their professional discipline was useless against her aggressive charm.

Driving on highways never excited Boo. When this was combined with her inability to sit still in a moving vehicle, she often became afflicted with bored restlessness. Days that languished through stagnant vistas were not her idea of a proper vacation. If herds of antelope appeared along the highway, I would feign excitement to tempt her interest. This usually inspired her to shift her body into a new position and groan.

But it was a different story when we pulled onto a dirt road surrounded by the sweet fragrance of pine and fir trees. With both front windows rolled down, she would balance her forepaws on the passenger-side window, whimper into the breeze, then bounce onto my lap and obscure my vision before returning to her side. This sequence could be repeated many times until I stopped and opened the door.

If we came upon a herd of cattle loitering on a country road, my copilot would put on her business hat and go to work. Crawling halfway through her window she would shame their insolence until the protesting cows cleared the road. Then continue to chastise them as they fell far behind us.

During another camping trip near Union Pass, we were driving to Moon Lake along a path that vaguely resembled a road. Boo hung onto her seat as if she were riding a bouncy ball down an uneven stairway. Tim and Darrin had taken the lead and were gradually getting farther ahead. A steady rain did nothing to assist our progress. At one point, the road pitched sideways and the truck felt like a sailboat without a keel. I was forced to steer toward the uphill side where a gnarly jumble of rocks sneered at us. When I tried to sneak below the sullen rock pile, my right rear tire slipped off the shoulder. The boys slowly disappeared into the clouds as I excavated piles of loose stones with my spinning wheels. We were officially stuck. I set the parking brake, turned the engine off, and blared my horn like a puny locomotive.

I hate doing nothing, so I had to do something. My plan was to stand in the rain and build a stone ramp where the tire had lost its grip. A shortage of rocks for my project wasn't an issue.

My plan also included restraining Boo with a doggy seatbelt. Although this thing had been stashed behind the front seat for several years, this was its first trial. I only wanted to keep her safe and dry.

The doggy seatbelt was a secure harness that anchored into the people seatbelt. I knew she would try to escape. She was already stretching her jaws toward the straps. To assuage her discomfort, I left her window open. By the time my ramp had grown into a small pile of three or four rocks, she was beside me and observing my slow progress. It was pointless to put her back in the truck, so we continued doing what we were doing and got soaking wet. I still have the doggy seatbelt and never bothered to use it again. It's undamaged and completely functional. I'll never know how she escaped from it.

I also had a doggy jacket in my truck, but there was no reason to dig it out. Boo could disrobe herself in less than one minute. I still have this accessory as well. Both items are in prime condition and available for a good price.

Our project was nearly finished when Tim and Darrin came back down the road. Although I was unable to test my off-road survival skills, the ramp was useful as Tim towed me onto the road. From there, we avoided additional mishaps while crawling through the rocks and rain.

Before having any concern about Boo and me, the Idaho boys had located a camping spot. It wasn't much farther up the road. For the remainder of the day, we sat under a holey tarp, drank beer, and told stories about extraterrestrials. Every now and then, we shifted our seats to avoid dripping water. Boo displayed a more refined intelligence and took full advantage of the vacant taco bed.

The next day, the sun came out. When our short hike ended along the banks of Moon Creek, Boo and I discovered lazy immobility. Fishing was less important than lounging with my girl along the shady creek. Sometimes adventure needs a day off.

Another time, back in Colorado, Boo was riding shotgun while we explored the backroads around Cheesman Lake. It was a wonderful summer day—until my battery died.

This happened a few years before the onset of my cell phone dependency. It was a desolate place for a breakdown and my impatience took control. We hiked down to the main service road where we hitched a ride to the mountain town of Deckers.

I didn't have a towing service in those days (although I've had one ever since). When I explained my situation to the guy at the Deckers store, he replied by pointing toward a wall bristling with business cards and assorted scribbled phone numbers. Then I mentioned my other problem and he pointed at a phone behind the counter.

There's nothing to do in Deckers. It's just a spot on the map with a couple of buildings, including the store. Language in this part of Colorado has been condensed into one or two necessary phrases, so I kept my shaggy dog stories to myself. For an hour or so, Boo and I sat on the store's porch, walked up and down the street, then returned to the porch while we waited for the tow truck.

When the tow truck arrived, the driver confirmed my identity, frowned at Boo, and grumbled, "The dog ain't ridin' in mah truck."

There was no way I was leaving Boo alone at the store. Following a short debate, I was granted a variance and lifted her onto my lap.

Back at my truck, the engine was still unresponsive as the driver tried to revive my battery. Our future was now bound to the conviction of this ornery autocrat. With deft maneuvering on the narrow road, he solemnly loaded my dead vehicle onto the bed of his tow truck. Once again, I was reminded about his no-dogs-in-the-truck policy.

"He'd be fine ridin' in yore car," he mumbled while acknowledging Boo with a stout, shop-stained finger. This covered the bulk of our conversation for the next few hours.

With Boo stowed in the front of my truck, we headed out on a sixty-mile excursion along winding mountain roads and across south Denver.

Through the rear window of the tow truck, I could see Boo's head whenever she was sitting up or standing. She seldom sat down, but she didn't appear anxious either. The elevated view must have been spectacular. Swinging back and forth between the driver's seat and the passenger seat, Boo piloted my truck on an unintended joy ride through the foothills of the Rockies.

This strange adventure may have been fun for her—and I certainly hope it was—but for me, it was worse than a totally wasted trip to the mountains. It was an expensive wasted trip. All the same, Boo finally got her chance to sit behind the wheel and fly down the road.

BACK TO THE FRONT

While I served my workday billable exile, Boo stayed with my mom at her house. She was Mom's dog during the day and my dog at night. Every morning, Boo and one of Mom's girls joined me to assess undeveloped property and get our blood flowing. Then I left the girls at Mom's house before heading off to earn my kibble.

On these days, my mom was also responsible for feeding Boo. I helped by keeping her pantry stocked with dog food. There was only one wrinkle with this arrangement: Mom's chow was better than mine. She always added goodies to Boo's dinner. These embellishments included hamburger, steak, gravy, and other delectable nibbles. When the weekend arrived, and after examining the tasteless grub I had lovingly prepared, she often preferred to starve.

Although impatience is Mom's primary motivational force, she is incredibly patient while training dogs. That's the key to developing a good companion. She can convince any pup to perform useful and silly tricks and has become fluent in several doggy dialects. While my mom is quite good at agility training, she excels at obedience training, which has never been in my bailiwick. With Boo and Koko, she achieved several titles in obedience.

Mom would use a covered parking lot at Walmart as a training space. Low-lit concrete caverns must be ideal for learning good behavior. I wouldn't recommend this, but it worked for her and the girls. The customers must have been intrigued by this crazy dog lady.

She loved Boo, and Boo loved her. My mom referred to Boo as "your daughter" whenever my girl had behaved unpleasantly. In other words, Boo's questionable upbringing was my fault.

Every day, Mom would take the dogs out for additional exercise. Yes, these girls were spoiled. Like me, she let them run off-leash, but she had a better excuse. One afternoon, Boo, Koko, Mom, and I were walking through an unfamiliar park. We obeyed the park's rules and had both girls on leashes. Koko disregarded her limited freedom, darted after a rabbit, and the whole side of Mom's face was dragged across asphalt pavement. While she didn't blame Koko, I had a few stern words for the little devil. Then there was another incident when Koko, once again restrained by a leash, charged toward a disrespectful mutt and sent my mom to the hospital. Mom was unable to accuse her puppy of any malice.

By the time she was two years old, Boo had become fairly reliable off-leash. I said "fairly," not "completely." She and I often walked across parking lots and along busy streets without a leash. Perhaps her loyalty was too strong to suspect otherwise. Or my complacency may have been related to simple luck.

Some things could short-circuit her reliability—with the obvious thing being coyotes. It was a late-winter day when Mom, Boo, and Koko took their usual walk around Bible Park. I was busy with work and spared from witnessing my worst nightmare. My mom was less fortunate.

As she had done many times before—as I had done many times before—Mom let the girls run freely around the park. Boo was seven years old, Koko was ten, and both had become trustworthy and dependable.

In the hierarchy of necessary behavior, priorities can overrule loyalty. As they proceeded down a path along Yale Avenue, Boo saw a coyote on the other side of the street.

When she raced into the street, a car ran over her. She went under the vehicle and reappeared as it passed over her. Somehow she had avoided being hit by the tires.

The driver stopped immediately and saved Boo from further injury. Whatever had been on this woman's schedule, Boo's rescue was now her primary concern. She was almost as devastated as my mom.

Having survived the lethal force of a moving vehicle, and while the driver managed passing traffic, Boo climbed to her feet and limped to the sidewalk where she left several bloody footprints. Then Mom, Boo, and Koko were loaded into the woman's car and returned to Mom's car. Once again, another angel came into our lives.

While cursing every idiot driver and stupid stoplight, Mom raced across south Denver until finally arriving at the Goldsmith Veterinary Clinic. As soon as Boo had been admitted, she called me and described the horrible event. Initially I thought Boo was gone, but she told me Sheila had survived and was in the trustworthy hands of Dr. Goldy.

I muddled through the rest of the workday as well as I could. Unsettled relief occupied my thoughts. Assured she was OK and receiving the best possible care, I worked until early evening then visited my parents to console my mom and say goodnight to the Monkey Girl.

After patching her up, Dr. Goldy didn't want to leave Boo at the clinic overnight (yes, another angel). To safely bring her to his home, he prepared a bed in the back of his SUV. Then he placed Boo on this bed, closed the hatch, walked to the front of the car, and opened the driver's-side door. That's when he discovered a dog, who was lucky to be alive, sitting in his passenger seat.

The next day, I visited Boo at the clinic. She weakly

acknowledged me. My strong girl was now fragile. I touched her as if she were a priceless China doll. She had fractured her wrist and had lacerations on her head. And she needed to pee. We took a short, slow walk around the icy parking lot. Very slow. She sat down several times before completing her task.

Dr. Goldy wanted to keep her for one more day. We were discussing her prognosis when he told me the passenger-seat story.

One week later, the bandage finally came off her wrist while she was chasing another coyote over at the Club.

TOYLAND

People love dogs because they love to play with us. They nurture and expose our inner child.

Young dogs will destroy anything that's within range of their stubby legs and tiny jaws. Toys allow them to develop this skill. Playing tug-of-war with our pups is not a competition of strength. This is how they engage us in total toy destruction. Their ancestors might have used a similar method for butchering and rendering their prey.

When Boo was young, I avoided the pricey pet shops and bought her toys at Walmart. Three Flippy Floppers at Walmart were the same price as a single flying toy at the pet store. Either gizmo had an expected lifespan of two weeks. When the aerodynamics were completely disabled, they became pull toys for another few weeks.

I also saved some cash by encouraging the girls to find their own toys. Although Boo wasn't prone to thievery, she did claim a few abandoned items. Yoshi, on the other hand, might assume ownership unless the other dog is bigger and more intimidating. If her guilt is obvious, I'll chase her down and make amends with the rightful owner. And when another felon scampers off with one of her possessions, it's my job to get it back.

Boo destroyed her playthings with surgical precision. If it was a squeaky toy, the source of the squeak would be extracted and dissected. And every little bit of stuffing was thoughtfully removed and spread around the house.

To entertain ourselves after a day of work, we played a game called "Mine!" To keep things fair, we usually played *boca a boca*. Boo was very possessive and would issue a cautious growl whenever I approached a hazardous situation. She could deliver several good nips in succession with her jaws snapping like a toothy sewing machine. As she swung her head around to deny my theft, I often intercepted her canines with my nose or forehead. She never intended to hurt me and if I started bleeding, she would calm down and start nursing my small wound. Then I would take advantage of her kindness by chomping down on the unattended toy and risk more punishment.

While traveling through uncultivated landscapes, Boo's possessiveness was a good thing. Her desire to carry her own toy absolved me of this burden. If our pace became dull and unfulfilling, she would throw her luggage at my feet, scream with authority, and make me toss it as far as I could.

There were times when her field work resulted in a lost toy. This often escaped my attention until we were well beyond where she had lost it. After I questioned its whereabouts, she would frown with self-annoyance before racing back to find it. Up to several minutes could elapse before she returned with the toy. Even though a few of these were written-off as donations, her retrieval record was outstanding.

Boo's daughter from another mother, Yoshi, is a natural capitalist. She enjoys and destroys her stuff much like any other dog. But she also understands that some toys are more valuable than others. Toys like shoes, slippers, books, TV remotes, and wallets are highly desirable because these can initiate endless chasing and human frustration.

As a puppy, Yoshi demolished anything, regardless of its value. Then she had a puppy epiphany. Some treasures had a longer useful life when not reduced to worthless scraps. If we showed any interest in her theft, she knew the negotiations would be in her favor. To avoid being trapped by her wiles, I would act indifferent if she eyed my two-hundred-dollar hiking boots. But my boots might have been quite chewy and tasty, so this was a dangerous gambit.

It wasn't long before all the chasing and swearing ended with a belly rub. While this concession didn't cure Yoshi's addiction to larceny, her criminal ambitions became less destructive.

She will also use rocks as currency. As a puppy, she would approach us with a small rock in her mouth. Then the stone was savored and ground against her teeth. We feared she might break a tooth or start a rock collection in her belly.

Our solution was to offer a treat to replace the rock. Perhaps it wasn't a giant leap of intuition, but before long, Yoshi began dropping stones at our feet with increasing frequency—preferably on a tile floor to ensure her request was heard. If she was ignored, she would pick it up, roll it around inside her mouth, then drop it again. She understood the value of persistence and human obedience.

The best toys are sticks. They're plentiful, disposable, and float better than the real thing. And I never had to buy or find a stick, it just magically appeared. Boo wanted to chase it and Yoshi wanted to be chased.

Whenever a stick is discovered, it cannot be left behind. Some dogs will grab the stick in the middle. Others will carry it by one end while proudly dragging the other end across the ground. The awkward imbalance that is preferred by the log draggers might result from eons of adaptation. When faced with the task of hauling mastodon bones or tree trimmings, wolves and their domesticated descendants understood the benefit of imbalance. This allowed them to travel through thick brush or doggy doors with minimal impedance and may explain how a large slash pile can migrate into the living room.

And when the prized piece of femur or lumber was dragged around in this manner, it became a useful weapon until the opponent claimed the opposite end. A snarling round of "Kill the Stick" would decide the rightful owner.

The best toys are reserved for Christmas. My family has a tradition of hanging doggy stockings during the holiday season. I'm not kidding; each one is embroidered with the dog's name. And these are not little pet stockings, but full-sized stockings filled with toys and treats and more toys and more treats.

Of course, doggies can't read their own names. It was common for one dog (like Boo) to lay claim to multiple Christmas stockings. As I've said, Boo wasn't a thief, but her understanding of sharing was not strong when treats were involved. That's when the humans would step in and play Santa's referee.

For most of my life, I've believed Christmas is also a doggy holiday. It's a day for celebrating the life of Jesus and a time for expressing gratitude for our dear companions. And, yes, a place at the table (or under the table) was always reserved for them when Christmas dinner was served.

MONTANA, AGAIN

I'm not a planner. Planning for my future begins about two days prior to the event. The only exception is planning for a vacation.

The annual vacation with the Idaho boys is preceded by months of illoquent emails, debatable memos, preliminary negotiations, multiple proposals, draft agreements, and a little progress. Our level of research would humble any renowned astrophysicist. And scheduling a vacation is a biblical effort that exceeds most congressional deliberations.

Before the age of instant gratification, Forest Service and USGS topographic maps were our primary references. Cabin reservations were locked in with phone calls and snail mail. Then we landed on Google Earth and made our reservations via the internet and email. We still haven't discovered the wonders of GPS and robo-navigators, so the old paper maps are still useful for finding destinations and getting lost.

Tim compiles additional background information such as fishing reports, stream flow data, road conditions, and miscellaneous tidbits. Hospitals and veterinary clinics are also identified in case something bad might happen.

I plan most of the cooking details. That's my job and I'm serious about it. My camp stove cuisine is not to be touched until I have granted this privilege. Nobody plans for cleaning up. That's why we bring an assortment of furry dishwashers.

Our camp is usually somewhere between Aurora and southwest Idaho. The mountain ranges bordering the Green River Basin in Wyoming have produced too many faded memories. This is the shortest drive for everyone and only requires eight-to-ten hours of brain-melting highway travel.

Montana often contends for the top spot in the vacation derby. Southwestern Montana has claimed victory in several planning debates. This demands more road-time on my end, but it's worth the additional fuel and patience.

When I was young and avoiding gainful employment, I spent a few years in Montana. For a year and a half, I was a lab technician on Flathead Lake where I supplemented my income with fresh trout, ruffed grouse, and a generous amount of road-kill venison. When the lack of a viable career entered my thoughts, I went back to school and attended Montana Tech in Butte.

While living in Montana, I was blessed with an expanse of wild country that was minutes away from anywhere. My rental home on Flathead Lake was less than a hundred yards from a national forest. I would knock on my neighbors' door and ask if I could hunt in their backyard. Even with my meager income, I enjoyed a wealth of wild adventure. One year, after summer school at Montana Tech, I hiked fifty miles through the Bob Marshall Wilderness. On the fourth day of this trip, I finally saw another person.

Montana is a haven for grizzly bears, mostly in the northwest where these bears mingle with Canadian cousins, and in the southwest around Yellowstone. While living there, I saw a few black bears but never a grizzly.

On my hiking trip through the Bob Marshall Wilderness, I followed some large grizzly tracks up a trail. My pursuit wasn't intentional. It was either follow the bear or add a day or two to my itinerary. The tracks were fresh and there was no evidence of any other critters between the bear and me. Being alone and unarmed, I slowed down. I was not eager to see the beast who had created these weighty impressions. As the sun dropped behind the Swan Range, I arrived at a fork in the trail. The bear had taken the western fork and I chose the other one. A mile or so later, I cautiously prepared my camp and tried to sleep while an invisible wild animal sniffed around my tent.

Whenever Boo and I visited Montana, the experience was often unforgettable. All the same, there is one memory that may refute my mental acuity. But it also recalls Boo's ridiculous amount of bravery.

It was a two-day drive to reach the planned rendezvous with Tim, Darrin, and another friend from Idaho, Bernie. On the first night, Boo and I camped in the Big Horn Mountains west of Sheridan, Wyoming. Even though there was a more direct route to our ultimate destination, the road through the Big Horns added some new country to my been-there-seen-that list.

On the following day, we drove down the western side of the mountain range and across one of those lonely and forgotten landscapes that are ubiquitous in Wyoming. This desolate road ended at Cody where I stopped at Sierra Trading Post to buy bear spray.

Before this trip, I had canvassed several sporting goods stores while searching for bear repellent. The only available facsimiles were those little pink pepper sprays for warding off urban predators. I was looking for something that would discourage massive intentions of savagery.

In Cody, I found the real thing and it was impressive. It looked like a small fire extinguisher and had a holster and a safety, just like a real firearm.

Our destination in Montana was grizzly bear country. In addition to adding bear spray to my standard camping list, I had also packed my .357. This caliber is not considered effective against an angry Ursus horribilis, but it added some firepower to my small arsenal.

From Cody, we leisurely traveled through Yellowstone with a large assembly of other modern pioneers. Then we abandoned our fellow travelers and crossed into Montana. A brief squall passed over our heads and we followed its muddy path to our planned rendezvous near Red Rock Lakes.

The Idaho boys were already two or three beers ahead of us. While I was digging around for my beer supply, Boo's sweetheart, Cliff, and another dog, Max, trotted over to pay their respects to the self-ordained princess. Boo responded by reminding them of their proper place.

Boo and Max had met on previous trips and had no love for each other. He was a bad-boy long-haired retriever who was related to Bernie. Max often tested Boo's castle doctrine and tufts of grey fur hanging from her mouth were proof of his guilt. I explained to Bernie that Boo was just flossing her teeth. He saw no humor in this.

The next day, we traveled to the West Fork Cabin in the hills north of Red Rock Lakes. This was a small Forest Service cabin with barely enough room for three men and two dogs (Bernie and Max had their own camper). If you search the internet for the West Fork Cabin, you might see my old skillet hanging above the wood stove. This wasn't a donation, but I hope it has been put to good use.

Following a night of large campfires and little sleep, we piled into Tim's truck and set out to find a fishing hole. Five minutes later, we came across two Forest Service rangers driving ATVs. To gain some local knowledge, we slowed down, stopped next to them, and introduced ourselves with a summary of our mission. The rangers didn't have any fishing advise but did inform us about a troublesome sow grizzly with two cubs. Despite having no specifics, they believed these bears could be somewhere nearby. A quick assessment of my possessions confirmed my suspicions. My bear spray and sidearm were safely concealed back at the cabin.

The rangers' concern was supported with additional information. The local whitebark pine trees were dying off and their seeds were an important food source for bears. In other words, the grizzly family was not only troublesome, but could have been hungry as well.

We thanked them for the warning and resumed our journey. A few bumpy miles later, nature was calling and I requested a rest stop. But this would have to wait until the road and terrain offered a suitable pull-off. A few minutes later, we drove past a dead cow with a severely mauled rear quarter. My valves were approaching failure when Tim finally found a place to stop. The condition of the road ahead of us looked questionable, so he turned his truck around before parking. In the distance, we could still see the ravaged cow.

Everybody got out. The boys and other dogs explored down the road while Boo and I claimed the territory behind the truck. As we were finishing our business, Boo raised her hackles and started barking toward the dead cow. I ordered her into the truck, jumped in behind her, and shut the passenger side door.

I was searching for any kind of weapon when Boo resumed her ranting. She was no longer inside the truck. The driver's-side door had been left open and Boo was standing in front of the truck where she was bad-mouthing a momma grizzly and two cubs. I should put quotes around "cubs." They were almost as large as their mother. These bears were standing behind a willow bush about fifty feet away from us. Their demeanor was more curious and confused than angry.

Compared to this hulking mass of bear-flesh, Boo looked like a vicious little bunny.

I shouted and whistled and she completed her lecture before jumping back into the truck. This time, I closed the driver's-side door, grabbed Boo's collar, and yelled through the open window, "Bear! Bear! Bear!" The windows were automatic and I had no choice but to leave them open. When I looked back toward the bears, they were gone.

At that point, it seemed more like a weird dream. There is a gap in my recollection. Somehow everybody reappeared safely back inside the truck. I was grateful nothing more than a bit of excitement had happened. The boys had also seen the grizzlies—except Bernie whose version of this encounter included a monstrous family of alpacas. As we drove up the road and past the dead cow, the bears reappeared and were retreating down to a small creek. There they paused and, with detached emotion, watched our departure.

These bears weren't the only grizzlies we saw on this trip. While in the safety of our trucks and traveling to a new campsite along the Ruby River, we passed a big boar and another sow with two small cubs. These bears were not far from where we had planned to camp.

Luckily there was a fishing hole next to our campsite and we never ventured far. Whenever Boo and I embarked on short excursions, I carried my bear spray on my belt and my .357 inside my pack. My fearless bear-alert system remained in standby mode and she was always within my sight.

Much to my relief, the rest of our vacation was relatively boring.

BODY LANGUAGE

Humans are quite dependent on vocal effluence but less reliant on sensible influence. All requests and demands are generated with chains of sounds that are strung together with, or without, emphasis. And these are resolved or denied with similar verbal constructions. Or silently ignored.

All the same, this preponderance of loquaciousness has its limits. A word on this side of the planet is meaningless on the other side. The only universal language is mathematics and nobody except engineers, accountants, researchers, and computer geeks care about math.

While dogs are quite verbose, physical communication is also important. Humans have not adapted to this type of social interaction because it might interfere with civility and, possibly, legality. We do not lick strangers' faces or sniff around their bodies. And we never pee in public if a signpost is begging for a response.

But in canine society, avoiding this behavior is proof of parental negligence.

Dogs could be telepathic as well. My mom subscribes to this theory and I've never proved her wrong. Their ability to control our thoughts transcends language and can be subtle or theatrical.

They often prefer physical and visual expressions for eliciting whims, wishes, doubts, and demands. Eye contact is extremely important. When dogs look at us, they want us to look at them. Then they will hold us in a trance until their demand is met. When a puppy discovers the effectiveness of his adorable eyes, he has found something more powerful than words.

Eye contact is how they seize our attention. Then the area around the eyes is used to build sentences. Their brows, lips, noses, and ears can be molded into myriad statements. Tails, hackles, and teeth can be used for punctuation.

Australian shepherds have naturally expressive eyes. Boo's contrasting light and dark eyes, set within an opposing shade of fur, lent a comical yet devilish duality to her expressions. The white side of her face with the brown eye was the joker half. The black side with the white eye was the troublemaker half.

And why do dogs wink? Whenever my stone-faced companion drops this subtle message on me, I'm not sure how to reply. If I respond with a wink, the only reaction is pure monk-like condescension.

Then there's the look-away—a deliberate avoidance of recognition. They don't have the ability to extend their middle fingers, but the chill of the look-away may be more effective.

And the side-eye always means trouble.

Tails prevent dogs from concealing their emotions. Most folks know how to read a dog's tail—if the dog has one.

Aussies are commonly known as "wiggle butts." This is how they compensate for their lack of a tail. Their tails are either naturally bobbed or have been deliberately removed (or "docked") soon after birth. To overcome this handicap and express happiness, Aussies must swing their backsides with exaggerated delight. It's similar to swinging a flyswatter instead of a baseball bat. And it's ridiculously endearing.

Boo's bobbed tail might have been natural. If not, she may have been raised by a well-intentioned breeder who docked all the puppies' tails regardless of their possible futures. Whatever the truth may be, she could shimmy like

Tina Turner when she greeted me after a day of work.

A dog's tail can also express other emotions. Concern will lower the tail. Apprehension will lower it further. And fear or submission will tuck the tail right under the belly.

Some dogs, like our Shibas, articulate their emotions with a full circle of tail-talk. This makes them the drama queens of the canine universe. With their tails curled tightly over their backs, they express pure confidence. When the tail goes straight out like a retriever's, they're in hunting or attack mode. If a Shiba's tail drops down, it can have several connotations. They might be relaxed or nervous. Their ears, face, and hackles will tell the rest of the story.

Most dogs are professional grinners. These contagious expressions are known to spread immediately and have no effective antidote. Their grins also suggest a sense of humor, comedy, and mischief.

A pup's smile is a sign of contentment. Yoshi smiles when there's nothing to worry about. Boo smiled when she slept. This lasted until she began growling at imaginary phantoms. If not sleeping or napping, she often had a big, laughing grin. I've always been a smiler, not a grinner, and this facial contortion was reserved for my semiannual bouts of good humor. After Boo came into my life, I finally learned how to expose my teeth during social gatherings.

Although Koko was a serious girl, she had a wonderful smile and reserved grin. On the other hand, whenever I took her into the hills, her broad grin would push the endurance of her cheek muscles.

A dog's physical communication also includes physical contact. Touchy-feely strangers make me nervous and as a rule, I avoid latching onto new acquaintances. But for our canine friends, this is acceptable behavior. They will engage us with their bodies, paws, chins, teeth, and, of course, tongues, while demanding absolute attention.

At the same time, it's not a good idea to touch a dog unless they have sanctioned this activity. They'll let us know if they're open to any back-scratching or butt-slapping. Many dogs are cautious around strangers. From my experience, most pups will require a sniff test before advancing to the touching phase. Then there are others, like Boo, who will plant their paws on anybody and give them a big hug.

While attending dog shows, our furry friends are discouraged from using their teeth on other warm-blooded objects. If someone's hand disappears inside their pet's mouth during a competition, the judge might disqualify the guilty team. But I've always allowed my dogs to do this because it's an important part of playtime and honest communication. As I see it, this develops a level of trust and allows my fingers to remain attached to my hand when I brush their teeth.

As everybody knows, a dog's communication skills are not limited to body language. They bark, yelp, yip, whimper, scream, shriek, moan, groan, growl, and howl, and create variations of these sounds that have multiple meanings.

I don't believe we have a word for it, but they commonly use a brief lilting sound if they are suffering from a lack of attention. It's like a tiny verbal nudge. Boo would use a similar, but more dramatic, "Ummmmph" when she lay down to relax. This translated as "Leave me alone" or "Good night." I've adopted this habit for myself whenever I need to expel tension or inquisitive strangers. It really works.

Yoshi will shake her dog tags to announce her presence. She also makes a squeaky noise when she yawns. It sounds like "Ar-yuh," and it means "Well? Are we just going to sit here and do nothing?"

Our furry friends must have a sense of vocabulary. This might seem obvious but let me continue. They can be trained to recognize and remember many words. Am I the only guy in the world who has to spell out W-A-L-K or B-U-N-N-Y so a dog won't understand me? I doubt it.

Even Yoshi understands words. Then she wiggles her ears to remove any remnants of what she had just heard.

Boo despised swear words and would frown at all my improper utterances. For her, listening was a precious gift from God, and bad language was a sacrilege.

I even tried to teach Boo how to count from one to five. If personal business forced me to abandon her for a few days, I would explain the length of my absence by counting the days on my fingers. She seemed to understand, and if the total count included my thumb, she would slouch with displeasure. But when we reunited, she would scream, wiggle, grin hugely, and wash my face.

SWEETWATER TO LABARGE

After traveling north through the middle of Wyoming, Boo and I stopped in Lander for gas, cell phone service, and last-minute supplies. Then we backtracked south before turning west along the road that led over South Pass.

The plan was to camp with Tim near the Sweetwater River on the other side of the pass. The day was winding down as the sun glared into our faces. After crossing the Sweetwater River, I turned onto the Lander Cutoff, flipped my sun visor toward the roof, and drove into the dry western foothills of the Wind River Range.

For eight miles, we sped across a well-graded unpaved road. My odometer combined with an ability to add numbers were the only clues for the turnoff. There were no street names or route numbers. This required a lengthy tour around a variety of backroads. On our map, these were identified with dotted lines that resembled a crazy quilt. Within an area of less than one square mile, we probably surveyed five miles before finding the predetermined campsite.

Thus far, I had honored our agreement, but Tim was absent and had yet to fulfill his portion of the contract. A smattering of phone calls and messages suggested he should have arrived hours before we did. I turned my engine off, Boo climbed down from my lap, and we stretched our legs in the remote silence. Five minutes later, she was quite puzzled when I lifted her into the truck and started the engine.

Daylight had been reduced to a tepid western glow and impatience was creeping in. We drove back to the main road—the Lander Cutoff—where a few bars of cell phone service were available. Tim didn't answer, so I left a message and prospected other likely camping spots before returning to the one we had agreed upon.

I repeated this routine several times while leaving a lengthy record of frustration and campsite travelogues on Tim's answering service. There was one location I hadn't investigated, even though it was not far from our camp. This spot had also been identified as a possible option, but it was already occupied by a large cluster of outdoor enthusiasts. Tim would have avoided this crowd. The proximity of strange neighbors inflicts him with severe discomfort. Official Forest Service campgrounds never enter our discussions about agreeable destinations.

As darkness settled in, it became obvious he was hopelessly lost. I abandoned my search and returned to our campsite. Then I dragged two huge green boxes out of my truck and prepared our sleeping quarters. As a beacon for my wayward fellow camper, my Coleman lantern was placed on the truck's roof.

It had been an exhausting drive to the southwest side of the Wind River Range. A failed and unplanned search-and-rescue expedition in the Sweetwater River backcountry had resulted in additional fatigue. Following a quick dinner of brats and kibble, I turned the lantern off and crawled into the taco bed with Boo.

The next morning, after finishing our breakfast, I saw a large patch of ground move beneath the sagebrush. The few beers I had enjoyed on the previous evening shouldn't have skewed my observations. Assured of my clarity, this phenomenon became more perplexing. I squinted and rubbed my eyes, but the ground continued to move. The sagebrush remained in place while their roots flowed toward the north.

We were camped along a small creek that fed into the Sweetwater River. Willows guarded the creek on one side of our camp and sagebrush extended to the horizon on the other side.

I alerted Boo about the migrating terrain. As she approached this impossible animation, the flowing ground transformed into a herd of sage grouse that burst into the air and flew to the far side of the creek. Although I should refer to this mass of birds as a flock or covey, the dense gathering of feathered critters resembled a herd—a herd of thirty-to-forty sage grouse.

Over the years, I have spent many miles and days exploring sagebrush country within the northwestern states. In all that time, and before this trip, I had only seen two sage grouse. These birds resemble small chickens and are classified within the same family as Poultrius edibilis. To see this large convention of eight-piece dinners was astonishing.

While most of the rivers on the western side of the Wind River Range flow west into the Green River or northwest toward the Snake River, the Sweetwater River is the only one that flows east.

Where we were camped—and where the Sweetwater River begins its unusual journey—the Continental Divide is a humble rocky outcrop that's west of the taller peaks. This low ridge nudges the river south, then east around the southern end of the mountains. There are elevated sections along this divide where numerous cell phone calls can be redialed and epic messages composed. Eventually, the Sweetwater River joins the North Platte River at Pathfinder Reservoir.

And, eventually, on the morning of the sage grouse

encounter, Tim found us. He had been camping, along with his dog, Zeke, right next to the camping cluster down below us. After witnessing the grouse herd, this was the second astonishing revelation of the day.

I congratulated Tim for finally arriving at the correct campsite. Then we jumped into his truck and bounced along miles of tortuous roads in the rocky foothills. For the entire day, we never touched our fishing gear. It was an atypical vacation day when fishing was less important than driving around giant lumps of granite that resembled stone-age fortresses. Captivating scenery or dead-end roads would halt our progress and allow me to recover from Boo's vigorous paw massages. Then we would crack open another beer.

The next day, we broke camp and followed Tim across the Green River Basin. Our next destination was the Scaler Cabin and LaBarge Creek. A series of unremarkable highways took us toward Kemmerer, which is strategically located in the middle of nowhere and globally renowned as the original home of the JC Penney enterprise. But we skipped the opportunity to visit this legendary outpost and turned north onto a rural road that led into the Salt River Range. This road ended at Fontenelle Creek and started again on the other side.

We forded the creek and washed the lower halves of our trucks before accumulating another layer of dirt. The road steadily degraded into an axel-grinding and pothole-infested trail. I was preoccupied with minimizing damage to my truck while Boo struggled to maintain a vertical position on her seat. She must have been questioning the need for this ruthless isometric workout.

The road continued to disintegrate while descending to LaBarge Creek. Along the creek we found a well-graded road that would have been a shortcut to Scaler Cabin, but this lacked the bone-jarring adventure of our first choice. A mile later we arrived at the cabin where we would enjoy a few days of rustic luxury.

I parked as close as possible to the front door, extracted two awkward green boxes from my truck, and rolled them inside. Then I threw my fishing gear into Tim's truck and we headed back out. As usual, Tim drove, I sat in the passenger seat, and Boo limited my comfort and view. Thankfully most of this trip was along the smooth road.

It had been a long hot day of nothing but driving. When Tim parked his truck along the creek, Boo was immediately drawn to the cool flowing water. Although it's called a creek, LaBarge Creek is more of a small river. Boo misjudged the depth and speed of the water and disappeared beneath the surface. Her head reappeared several feet from the undercut riverbank. She furiously clawed against the strong current and narrowed the distance between us. I threw myself to the ground with my arms reaching over the riverbank, grabbed her scruff, and pulled her out. If this had failed, I would have jumped in to save her. The risk was inconsequential—Boo was my child. For the rest of the afternoon, she didn't go near the creek.

The next day, we explored Notellum Creek—a small tributary to LaBarge Creek. This stream was a haven for trout and graced the most picturesque setting I have ever seen. The quality of the fishing almost took second place to the pure aesthetics of this beautiful spring creek as it flowed over flat terraces separated by vertical waterfalls.

Over the years, I've read many fishing stories and our streamside preferences may require clarification. According to angling literature, people who fish together always fish together—I mean right next to each other. When Tim and I fish together, we agree on a vague time and location for meeting up then disperse in opposite directions. And when we fish together with Darrin, we play a game called "Where's Darrin?" Sometimes this game does not end until well after dark. It simply makes sense to spread out and respect each other's space—unless your dog prefers to fish with the other person.

Although I caught several nice trout on Notellum Creek, my efforts were interrupted by my desire to keep Boo nearby. How many times did I hike up the creek to find my loyal companion? More than a few. Each time, I found her chumming with Tim and Zeke and would remind her about our loose definition of "togetherness." With a hint of disinterest, she would accept my reasoning, follow me down the creek, and trot back to Zeke and Tim once my line hit the water.

On the final morning of our vacation, Boo confirmed her true faithfulness. Tim and I were relaxing on the porch, chewing on coffee grounds, and taking a break from our chores. Boo was nowhere in sight, but I wasn't worried. She and Zeke often explored the area near the cabin and came back when their surveys were completed.

Tim and I were reminiscing about past adventures and planning future trips when we heard a rhythmic squeaking sound coming from Tim's truck as it rocked from side to side. A mysterious invisible force was making the truck sing and dance. It was almost as haunting as the breakfast medley surprise that was growling inside our bellies. Paranormal activity was the obvious answer. A few lost souls may have been left behind after years of logging, mining, hunting, and gathering. A more thorough investigation was necessary.

When we walked around Tim's truck, we found an open door on the driver's side. Boo had both front paws planted on the running board and was desperately trying to jump into Tim's truck. The persistent rhythm of her hopping and pushing showed her determination. Although she wasn't a puppy anymore and years had passed since she could leap into Tim's truck, the allure of more backcountry adventure was too powerful.

Two hefty and heavy green boxes were waiting to be loaded into my truck and I was almost ready to start the trip back home. Somehow this must have escaped her attention.

TIDBITS

I had two stories that were too short to stand on their own and couldn't be shoehorned into any of the previous stories or essays. But they add a little more to Boo's character and there may not be another opportunity to share them.

Friday night is when I usually visit my mom (or both my parents before my dad passed away). This gathering includes dining on takeout food while watching *The X-Files* or *Star Trek* DVDs. After dinner (and another incredible victory for the USS *Enterprise*), the girls and I would excuse ourselves for an evening walk around the neighborhood. It's a tradition that began with Nahni and Koko and continues with Yoshi by my side.

The neighborhood is quiet and civil, but it has its share of idiot drivers. With this in mind, I've always kept the girls on leashes—well, almost always.

Our route goes down Olive Street to Mansfield Avenue, over to Oneida Street, up to Eastmoor Drive, back across Olive, and then, finally, back to my parents' house. This may sound like a boring routine, and sometimes it is, but the girls have always enjoyed it.

At one time, a raccoon family lived inside a storm sewer on Olive Street. Their front door was a cast-iron grate that was set into the gutter. The girls would pull hard on their leashes until we arrived at the grate, then sniff around the premises to see if anyone was home.

These were the neighborhood raccoons and my mom would leave treats for them in her backyard. The big fat one was named "Rudy." He might have been counted as another pet, but as long as the girls had veto power, Rudy would never achieve full membership in our family.

Whenever they visited—and while Boo and Yoshi were settled inside my folks' house—Rudy and his clan would climb down from their tree and grab a snack. If either girl detected the intruders' presence, the other would be alerted and both would scramble through the dog door and warn the entire neighborhood about the raccoon invasion.

After pulling the girls away from the storm sewer, we would resume our walk while stopping every twenty feet to sniff or pee. One night, during the holidays, the Monkey Girl relieved herself on a Christmas deer that was glittering with electric lights. Like a boy dog, she lifted her leg and aimed at the deer's hind quarter. And she survived.

As Boo matured, I got lazy and stopped using her leash during these walks. We had completed this same circuit hundreds of times. She was also becoming a slow reader and we made better time if I continued down the sidewalk with Yoshi. Boo would soon notice our departure and catch up with us.

Oneida Street has always had the worst traffic in this neighborhood. This is a known shortcut for reckless NASCAR wannabes.

One Friday evening, as we were heading up Oneida, Yoshi left a fertile donation in the shadows of someone's front yard. Boo was fifty feet behind us and engaged in personal research. It took a while to find Yoshi's charitable deposit. When I finally had it bagged and tagged, Boo had disappeared.

Yoshi and I walked up and down the street several times. I strained my eyes toward every dark obstruction while hoping Boo would emerge and trot back to us. It was hard not to panic. My control of everything had slipped away. At the same time, I knew she was not lost. This was her domain. Then I switched to Plan B and called my mom.

"I've lost Boo! She was with me, then she wasn't."

"She's right here at the front door. Where are you?"

When Boo was ten years old and had not competed in agility for over five years, I submitted entry forms for two agility trials: a NADAC trial and an ASCA trial. This impulse wasn't a desire to ignite my old obsession, I only wanted to display my girl's talents a few more times before she was too old to compete.

Fortunately, I had enough sensibility to check the rules for any updates. During the intervening years, NADAC had introduced a new obstacle called a "hoop" which was a Hula-Hoop that stood perpendicular to the ground. The idea was to guide the dog through the hoop. It resembled a jump with a curved bar on the top. Or might have been mistaken for a thin version of a "tire" obstacle, except tires were elevated above the ground. The hoop sat at ground level and the dog simply ran through it. This sounds easy, but it took a while for Boo to associate this new thing with a new command: "Hoop!"

This project required buying two Hula-Hoops and jerry-rigging frames to hold them in a vertical position. Over the years, my mom and I had acquired a variety of agility obstacles that we kept in her backyard. I experimented with different layouts to rekindle Boo's athletic skills and acquaint her with the hoops. Training revitalized our competitive spirit and I had forgotten how good she was.

Because of her age, Boo competed as a veteran novice dog in both trials. This had a couple of benefits: the jumps would be sixteen inches high (instead of twenty) and there would be a limited number of dogs to compete against.

I wish someone had captured these runs on video. Her performances were nearly flawless, even with gritty winds blasting across the courses at the ASCA trial. Our only mistake was my mistake when I sent her over the wrong obstacles during a gamblers run. Following my misguided advice, she tackled the more challenging non-novice gamble, which she completed perfectly. Her skills were still excellent and she raced through the hoops like a true veteran. It was silly, wonderful, and fun.

The results of these two trials were seven qualifying runs and five first places. If we had continued to pursue this agility revival, it's possible she could have earned new titles by the end of summer. But I was satisfied with her performances and we went back to being dogs again. There would be no more agility events, but there would be many adventures in the days ahead.

EPILOGUE—THOUSANDS

When I said goodbye to Boo, I wanted to write an essay about her life and post it on Facebook. Then all my Friends might read it and discover what an incredibly awesome girl she had been. I started with a single word with weighty implications: "Thousands." I gave up on the Facebook essay when my efforts exceeded the limits of social media.

I don't have thousands of human friends. Not even a hundred. Maybe not even ten. The folks and pups whom I have mentioned in the previous stories are my friends and I have a few more who knew and loved Boo.

This title arose when I realized Boo and I had traveled thousands of miles together while walking, wading streams, hiking, and running around agility courses. On my two feet and her four paws, we had covered a distance that would have taken us from California to New York. Maybe farther.

Every day included at least two walks and the total distance was at least one mile. I'm not including any of Boo's detours, which would have doubled this figure. Each year we would have traveled at least 365 miles (or 366 miles during leap years). Then the number just keeps growing.

The days we had together numbered in the thousands. As does the number of days when my mom cared for her.

The tally for every excursion where nothing notable, exciting, or terrifying happened was in the thousands. And I'm thankful for this.

Beggar's-ticks are small seeds with Velcro-like shells. Beggars probably can't afford real ticks and these obnoxious seeds might be a cheap alternative. The plants that produce these tiny pests live in swampy areas. Boo was quite familiar with their habitat. I removed thousands of beggar's-ticks from her coat. It's actually a simple process: use a wide-toothed comb and be ready to get nipped if you pull too hard.

Throughout her life, her nose color transformed from completely pink to totally black. Thousands of coats of sunscreen may have helped this.

Keeping with this theme, I began to wonder about other things in Boo's life that could be measured in quadruple digits.

We didn't encounter thousands of coyotes, but this number was well over a hundred. There were times when it was a nightly occurrence.

Boo's possessions included only a hundred or so toys, but this was still impressive.

Awards earned from agility trials have been boxed up and tucked away inside my attic. This record of achievement includes nearly a hundred ribbons and a few title certificates. Miles driven to agility training and trials was easily in the thousands. Dollars spent in this endeavor? Yes, thousands.

One day, after an agility competition in Wyoming, my mom, Koko, Boo, and I visited a nearby state park. As soon as the car door opened, both girls spotted a group of bunnies and chased them into a thick cactus patch. Over the following days, we probably pulled hundreds of thorns from their feet. It was almost as bad as when Mom's huskies, Sasha and Tamara, ran into the wrong end of a porcupine.

I have a camping checklist with over a hundred items. Only fifteen of these were for Boo. Most of this stuff fit inside her beach bag. And she never complained about the economy of her camping necessities. The escape from civilization was more than sufficient for her happiness.

Picking up Boo's poop with a plastic bag was initially an

act of bravery. She was not discrete about her business and this forced me to adapt. Years later, I was a seasoned pro who had properly disposed thousands of poop bags. I had become a connoisseur. Some bags are excellent, some are good, and others aren't worth the poop I put in them.

Accounting for kisses is difficult. This would have been somewhere north of a hundred for every month. Each one should have its own memory but there were too many. When considering this amount of facial bathing, we probably shared similar strains of microflora. Whenever she farted, I wasn't sure whether I wasn't the culprit.

Most of the thousands of muddy footprints have been scrubbed or swept clean. I hope a few of these are still hiding somewhere inside my house.

Boo shed her coat constantly. I'm not allergic to dog hair but I have bad reactions to housecleaning. I learned to live with it. White fur was incorporated into everything I owned and ate. I seldom gave her a bath and this was not necessary. She wore a new coat every week and left her old one inside my car, on my bed, and all over my rugs. Sometimes I invited my friend—and Boo's best friend—Kelly to come over and clean my house. After a day of vacuuming, Kelly collected enough fur to cover a Saint Bernard. Millions of hairs were shed throughout her life.

Over the years, thousands of smudges—or nose art—covered the right side of the windshield and the passenger-side window. I cleaned these whenever visibility became limited.

And the thousands and thousands of times when I whispered, said, shouted, or screamed, "Sheila," "Boo-boo," "Boo," "Princess," or "Puppy Girl" are still echoing in the stars.

ACKNOWLEDGEMENTS

I've used a lot of fancy words while composing these stories and essays. For example, I owe a prodigious amount of thanks to those folks and puppies who were responsible for this journey.

Many of them have been included in these stories and I won't repeat their names again. Once or twice was probably enough to compromise our relationships. And I promise to keep their identities confidential.

Without Tim's scribbled list of our annual camping trips, my recollections would have been complete fiction. At the same time, these might include a touch of creative license.

My façade of erudition was enabled by professional help. Josh Phillips with the Cherry Creek/High Line Canal Conservancy took time to enlighten me about the history of Denver's eastern water supplies. And Darrel Dunn did his best to unravel my misconceptions about the geology of the Denver Basin.

If the day ever arrives when I can call myself a writer, it will happen because of Elisabeth Chretien and her zombies.

My sister gave me the willpower to push through those days when every sentence looked like a garbled mess. And the love of her life, Andy, supported my writing by simply enjoying it.

Without my mom, there would have been nothing to write about.

And I thank God for sending a true angel when I truly needed one.